KU-314-085

Cordon Bleu

Cooking from Abroad

Cordon Bleu

Cooking from Abroad

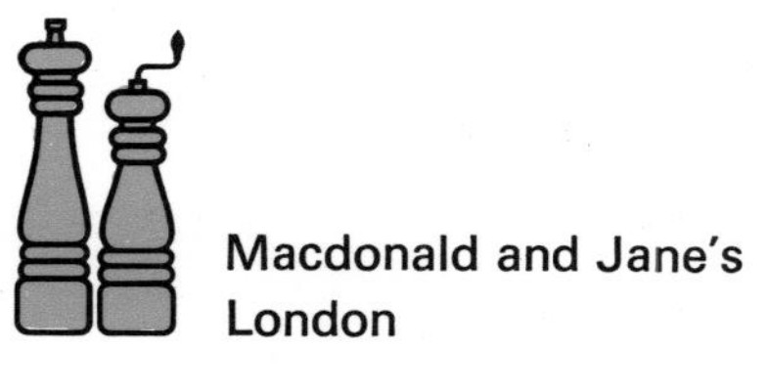

Macdonald and Jane's
London

Published by
Macdonald and Jane's Publishers Ltd
Paulton House
8 Shepherdess Walk
London N1

This impression 1977

Designed by Melvin Kyte
Printed by Waterlow (Dunstable) Ltd

These recipes have been adapted from the Cordon Bleu Cookery Course published by Purnell in association with the London Cordon Bleu Cookery School
Principal : Rosemary Hume ; Co-Principal : Muriel Downes
Quantities given are for 4 servings.
Spoon measures are level unless otherwise stated.

Contents

Introduction

One of the most exciting things about eating is experimenting with new tastes. There is nothing wrong with traditional English dishes, and most of us love to eat them most of the time. But there comes a moment when a touch of the unusual is called for – whether it be to encourage a jaded palate, to impress an important guest, or simply to give the cook a change. That's what this book is all about.

We have collected together all sorts of recipes, from western Europe where you have probably picked up a few holiday favourites yourself and from further afield. One point though – adaptation has played an important part in these recipes. We felt it was no use giving recipes which included ingredients that are almost impossible to come by in this country, neither was there much point in producing authentic flavours that none of our readers would stomach. So our recipes do not claim to be more than Cordon Bleu variations on the original material. We hope they are still delicious, but be wary of serving them to nationals of the country concerned – you are likely to produce nothing more than a yearning to return to mother's home cooking !

That warning apart, we hope to take you on a gastronomic journey round the world that will cater for most occasions, whether you choose a peasant goulash from Hungary, a delicious pigeon dish from Scandinavia or a deep south apple pie from the USA. Methods of cooking remain much the same, whatever the materials, so experienced cooks will not have much difficulty in following the recipes. As usual, though, we have included an appendix of basic recipes and notes on items that recur throughout the book, and a glossary of the cooking terms used. We hope that this will provide all the information that the less practised among you will require.

If cooking were a chore to you, you probably wouldn't be reading this book anyway. But certainly one of its effects could be to remove for ever the last traces of monotony from the kitchen. If experiment is fun for the diner it is doubly fun for the cook.

Rosemary Hume
Muriel Downes

Western Europe

So near and yet so far, gastronomically western Europe has much to offer the British appetite. Basic foodstuffs are very similar to our own, with the exception of some vegetables which thrive in the mediterranean countries but are expensively imported here, but methods of preparation are different. In addition, the rest of Europe has not been so much affected as we have by American methods of food production, processing and packaging.

Where the British might eat frozen New Zealand lamb and frozen peas or brussels sprouts, the German equivalent is more likely to be salt meat – probably pork – and sauerkraut, while the French have more ready access to the rich mixture of southern vegetables that make up a ratatouille. On the dessert side, the Austrians come into their own, with delicious gâteaux and curd cakes. Italy can compete on any front while Switzerland and Spain have their own specialities that anyone who has been there will want to repeat at home.

Wiener schnitzel

4–5 thin escalopes (measuring about 5 inches by 3 inches)
seasoned flour
1 egg (beaten, seasoned and 2–3 drops of oil added)
dry white breadcrumbs
clarified butter, or a mixture of oil and butter (for frying)

For garnish
1 lemon (sliced)
capers
gherkins (sliced)

To finish
1–2 oz butter
juice of 1 lemon
chopped parsley

To prepare escalopes: lay the slices of veal fillet between waxed or greaseproof paper and beat well to make them thin and flat.

If the veal is properly prepared by the butcher, it should not be necessary for you to beat them.

Method

Roll the escalopes in seasoned flour, shake, brush with egg and roll in the crumbs, pressing them on well.

Heat the butter in a large frying pan, put in the escalopes and fry over a moderate to slow heat for about 7–10 minutes, turning once only. Place veal on a hot flat dish, garnishing the middle of each schnitzel with a slice of lemon topped with capers and gherkins. Keep warm while preparing the butter.

Wipe out the pan, reheat and drop in the 1–2 oz butter. Cook to a noisette (until nut-brown), add lemon juice and pour over the escalopes just before sending to table. Dust with chopped parsley and serve at once.

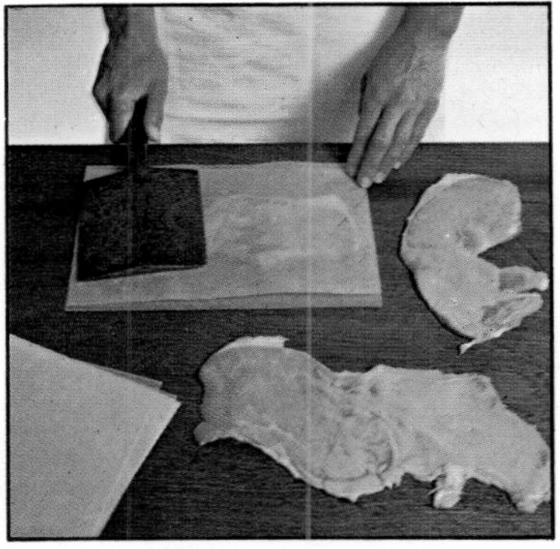

Beating out escalopes from veal fillet slices with a cutlet bat

Chicken Marengo

1 roasting chicken (weighing $2\frac{1}{2}$–3 lb)
1 tablespoon oil
2 oz clarified butter
2 large ripe tomatoes
1 clove of garlic (crushed with a little salt)
1 tablespoon tomato purée
1 wineglass white wine
$\frac{1}{2}$ pint demi-glace sauce
12 small button mushrooms
chopped parsley

To garnish
1 small egg per person
1 heart-shaped croûte per person
1 crayfish tail per person
little chicken stock

Method

Cut the chicken as for a sauté, heat the oil, add the butter and put in the chicken, skin side down; cook slowly until golden-brown on both sides. Remove from the pan, cover and keep warm.

Tip the fat from the pan and keep it on one side to cook the croûtes and eggs. Scald and skin the tomatoes, cut them in four, squeeze out the seeds and chop the flesh. Put these in the sauté pan with the garlic and tomato purée. Cook over a gentle heat until well blended, add the white wine, and reduce to half quantity. Pour on the demi-glace sauce, add the mushrooms, replace the chicken, cover and simmer gently until tender (about 25–30 minutes). Fry the croûtes and the eggs in the reserved fat. Take up the chicken, arrange in the middle of a flat round dish and spoon over the sauce. Dip the tip of each croûte in a little sauce and then in chopped parsley. Arrange croûtes round the dish and put a fried egg on each one; place a crayfish tail, previously heated in a spoon or two of the stock, between each.

It is said that this dish was created after the battle of Marengo when Napoleon's chef gathered all the ingredients he could find into one dish

Griestorte with pears

3 eggs
4 oz caster sugar
juice and grated rind of ½ lemon
2 oz fine semolina
½ oz ground almonds

For filling
¼ pint double cream
½ teaspoon caster sugar
1–2 drops of vanilla essence
3 ripe dessert pears

To finish
icing sugar
chocolate (finely grated) – optional

8-inch diameter sandwich tin

In this light but short-textured cake, fine semolina is used instead of flour. This cake keeps better than a sponge and marries well with different fruits. The proportions given make a cake to serve 8 people.

Method

Butter the bottom of the sandwich tin and line with a disc of greaseproof paper; butter the greaseproof paper and sides of the tin, dust first with caster sugar, then flour. Set oven at 350°F or Mark 4.

Separate egg whites from yolks; work yolks and sugar together in a bowl with a wooden spoon until light in colour. Then add lemon juice and continue beating until thick. Stir in grated lemon rind, semolina and ground almonds. Whisk egg whites in a bowl to a firm snow and fold into mixture with a metal spoon. Turn into prepared tin, bake in pre-set oven for 40–50 minutes.

If using an electric mixer, the best result is obtained by beating together the yolks, sugar and lemon juice until very thick. Stir in the dry ingredients as above and leave mixture standing while egg whites are whisked by hand with a balloon whisk. This stops any grittiness in the finished cake.

The mixture will rise a great deal but also subside. This is quite in order but do not open oven door until cake has been baking at least 25–30 minutes.

When the cake is cold, split and fill with sweetened whipped cream, flavoured with vanilla essence, and sliced pears. Dust top with icing sugar, and decorate with chocolate.

Austrian coffee cake

6 oz butter
6 oz caster sugar
3 eggs (beaten)
6 oz self-raising flour
pinch of salt
$\frac{1}{2}$ pint strong black coffee
sugar and rum or brandy (to taste)
$\frac{1}{2}$ pint double cream (whipped)
1–2 drops of vanilla essence
almonds (browned)

Ring mould ($1\frac{1}{2}$ pints capacity) or 8-inch diameter cake tin

Method

Set the oven at 375°F or Mark 5. Cream the butter in a bowl, add the sugar, and cream again until light and fluffy. Beat in the eggs a little at a time and lastly fold in the sifted flour and salt with a metal spoon. Turn the mixture into the greased ring mould and bake for about 25 minutes, or 35–40 minutes if using a cake tin.

When cooked, take cake out of oven, remove from mould and set aside to cool. When cold return to mould. Sweeten the coffee to taste, and flavour with rum or brandy. Pour slowly over cake while still in mould. Coat with the cream, sweetened and flavoured with vanilla essence. Decorate with the browned almonds.

Austrian coffee cake is one of the more decorative sweets. The cake is soaked in sweetened coffee that has been flavoured with rum or brandy; it is then covered with vanilla-flavoured whipped cream and browned almonds

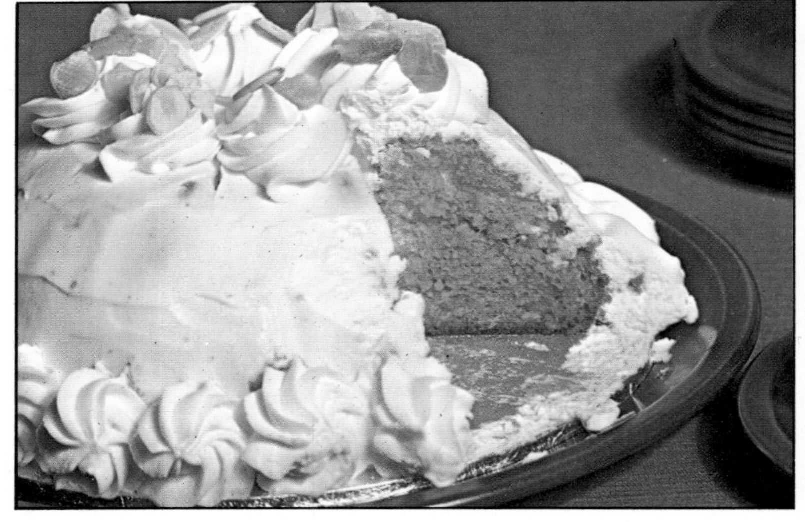

Austrian cheese cakes

6 oz plain flour
4 oz butter
2 oz ground almonds
3 oz dry Cheddar cheese (grated)
salt and pepper
1 egg yolk
1 dessertspoon water
beaten egg
Parmesan cheese (grated)

For filling
$1\frac{1}{2}$ oz cheese (grated)
$\frac{1}{4}$ pint milk
1 teaspoon arrowroot
salt and pepper
1 teaspoon paprika pepper
1 egg (separated)

1–$1\frac{1}{2}$-inch diameter plain cutter

Method

Sift flour, rub in butter very lightly. Add almonds, cheese and seasoning. Bind with egg yolk and water if necessary. Chill for 15 minutes.

Set oven at 375°F or Mark 5. Roll out to about $\frac{1}{8}$ inch thick and stamp into rounds about 1–$1\frac{1}{2}$ inches in diameter. Brush half of these with beaten egg and sprinkle with Parmesan cheese. Place on baking sheets lined with greaseproof paper and bake in pre-set oven for 10–12 minutes until golden-brown. Allow to cool.

Meanwhile prepare filling: mix all the ingredients together adding the egg yolk and reserving the white. Bring slowly to the boil, stirring all the time. When at boiling point, draw aside. Whisk white to a firm snow and fold into the hot mixture. Bring again to the boil and turn out to cool.

Sandwich the rounds together with a good teaspoon of the filling, using the plain round as the base.

Viennese curd cake

12 oz curd cheese
about 6 oz semi-sweet biscuits
$1\frac{1}{2}$ oz butter
$4\frac{1}{2}$ oz granulated sugar
3 egg whites
scant $\frac{1}{2}$ oz gelatine (soaked and dissolved in 2 tablespoons water)
2–3 drops of vanilla essence
$7\frac{1}{2}$ fl oz double cream (lightly whipped)

8-inch diameter flan ring

Method

Butter the inside of the flan ring. Crush biscuits, melt butter and stir in the biscuit crumbs with 1 oz of the sugar. Put half of this mixture at the bottom of the flan ring. Cream the curd cheese and the remaining sugar together, whisk the egg whites until stiff. Beat dissolved gelatine into curd and sugar mixture, add vanilla essence. Fold in cream and egg whites. Pour into flan ring, smooth the top and cover with rest of the crumbs. Leave to set. Serve with an apricot sauce.

Apricot sauce

Simmer about $\frac{1}{4}$ lb dried apricots until tender (in the water in which they were soaked overnight – about $\frac{1}{2}$ pint) with a strip of lemon rind. Then rub apricots through a strainer or sieve. Sweeten to taste and thin sauce a little with water, if necessary.

Braised beef flamande
with tomato coulis

$2\frac{1}{2}$ lb joint of topside beef
2 tablespoons dripping
plate of mixed root vegetables (sliced)
$\frac{1}{4}$ pint brown ale
$\frac{1}{4}$ pint brown stock
bouquet garni
1 teaspoon tomato purée
kneaded butter, or 1 dessertspoon arrowroot (slaked with 1 tablespoon cold water)
chopped parsley

For tomato coulis
1 lb tomatoes (skinned, seeds removed and sliced)
1 Spanish onion (sliced in rings)
1 tablespoon oil, or dripping
salt and pepper

Coulis is French for a soup stew or liquid thickened with pieces of vegetables or meat.

Method

Brown the joint of beef all over in the hot dripping in a flameproof casserole. Take out the meat, put in the prepared vegetables, cover and sweat them for 7 minutes. Then replace the meat, pour round ale and stock, add bouquet garni and tomato purée. Cover tightly and braise in the oven, set at 325°F or Mark 3, for about $1\frac{1}{2}$ hours or until tender.

When beef is cooked, make the tomato coulis. Fry the onion rings until just brown in the dripping in a frying pan, then add the prepared tomatoes. Season, cover pan and cook for 2–3 minutes only until tomatoes are just soft.

Slice the beef, strain gravy and thicken with kneaded butter or arrowroot. Dish up tomatoes and arrange slices of beef on

top, spoon over a little of the gravy and serve the rest separately. Dust well with parsley.

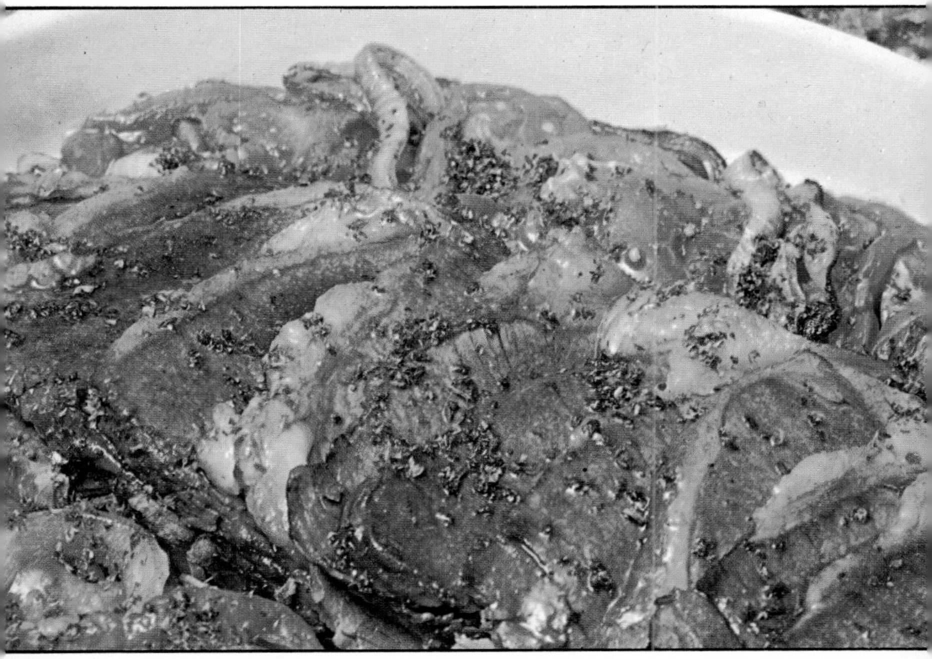

Serve with carrots and creamed potatoes.

Chicken waterzoi

1 roasting chicken (weighing 3 lb)
3 young carrots
1 medium-size onion
2 leeks
1 oz butter
salt and pepper
pinch of sugar
2 wineglasses white wine
4 parsley roots (Hamburg parsley if possible)
$\frac{1}{2}$–$\frac{3}{4}$ pint chicken stock
2 teaspoons arrowroot
2 egg yolks
3–4 fl oz double cream
chopped chervil and tarragon

This dish is Flemish in origin and the name is derived from waterzootje, which is in fact a fish dish, but chicken waterzoi is prepared in the same way.

Method

Set oven at 350°F or Mark 4.

Cut the vegetables in julienne strips. Melt half the butter in a small flameproof pan and add the vegetables; cover and cook for 1 minute, then season lightly and add the sugar. Pour over 1 glass of wine and bring to the boil; cover with a buttered paper and lid and cook in pre-set moderate oven until the wine has evaporated (about 10 minutes).

Wash and scrape the parsley roots well and tie them together with string. Season inside the bird with salt and pepper and truss neatly. Rub the remaining butter round the sides of a deep flameproof casserole, put in the chicken, pour over the rest of the wine and the stock and set the parsley roots alongside. Season with salt and pepper and scatter the vegetables over the chicken; cover with a buttered paper and close-fitting lid and bring to the boil. Turn the oven down to 325°F or Mark 3 and cook the chicken until it is very tender (about 1–1$\frac{1}{2}$ hours).

Take up the chicken, cut it into neat joints and arrange in a deep serving dish. Lift out the parsley roots, rub them through a wire strainer and return this purée to the casserole. Mix the arrowroot with the egg yolks and add the cream; stir this into the vegetables and stock, add herbs and cook gently until sauce coats a wooden spoon. Taste for seasoning and spoon sauce over chicken.

Garbure paysanne

1 medium-size turnip
2 medium-size carrots
$\frac{1}{2}$ small cabbage
2 medium-size onions
2 leeks (white part only)
1 small head of celery
2 medium-size potatoes
3–4 oz butter
1 cup cooked haricot beans
3–4 pints water, or stock
1 French roll, or small croûtes of bread
1–2 oz Gruyère cheese
salt and pepper

Garbure, one of the classic soups of France, is a rustic or peasant vegetable soup, thick and substantial, so much so that it is frequently eaten as a main dish. A garbure is characterised by the croûtes of bread which are browned in butter and put on top of the soup before serving, or are served separately. The ingredients of garbure vary, as does the finishing of the croûtes, and this depends on where the garbure is made. For example, in the southern provinces, the croûtes are not always browned but are layered into the garbure.

The following recipe is perhaps the most classic.

Method

Finely slice the raw vegetables. Choose a large stew pan, melt 1 oz butter in this and put in all the vegetables except the beans. Cover the pan and cook slowly for 15–20 minutes; the vegetables must not brown. Add the beans and a good 2 pints of the water (or stock); this should well cover the vegetables – add more if necessary. Cover pan and simmer until vegetables are really tender.

Cut the French roll into croûtes and fry in 1 oz of the butter until golden-brown; set aside.

Take out 3 tablespoons of the vegetables with a draining spoon and pass them through a sieve or blender, then put in a pan with the remaining butter and cook until the consistency of mashed potato. Spread this purée over the croûtes, doming it up and grate over the cheese. Set croûtes on a baking sheet and put to brown in a moderately hot oven.

Meanwhile put the rest of the soup through a sieve or blender; add the remaining water (or stock) and continue to simmer until it becomes a smooth purée. Season well and, if wished, add a further ounce of butter in small pieces. Serve the soup very hot with the croûtes floating on top or served separately on a plate.

Quiche lorraine

For rich shortcrust pastry
6 oz plain flour
pinch of salt
3 oz butter, or margarine
1 oz shortening
2 tablespoons cold water

For filling
1 egg
1 egg yolk
1 rounded tablespoon grated cheese
salt and pepper
$\frac{1}{4}$ pint single cream, or milk
$\frac{1}{2}$ oz butter
2–3 rashers of streaky bacon (diced)
1 small onion (thinly sliced), or 12 spring onions

7-inch diameter flan ring

Hot or cold, this egg and bacon tart is a typical dish from the Lorraine region of France.

Method

Make the rich shortcrust pastry (see right) and set aside to chill.

When chilled, line the pastry on to the flan ring. Beat the egg and extra yolk in a bowl, add the cheese, seasoning and cream or milk. Melt the butter in a small pan, add the bacon and sliced onion, or whole spring onions, and cook slowly until just golden in colour. Then turn contents of the pan into the egg mixture, mix well and pour into the pastry case.

Bake for about 25–30 minutes in an oven at 375°F or Mark 5.

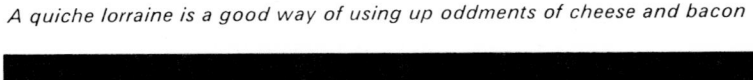

A quiche lorraine is a good way of using up oddments of cheese and bacon

Pissaladière

For rich shortcrust pastry
8 oz plain flour
pinch of salt
4 oz butter
2 oz shortening
1 egg yolk
2 tablespoons cold water

For filling
1 lb onions (thinly sliced)
4 tablespoons olive oil
12–15 black olives
2 teaspoons French mustard
6–8 tomatoes (skinned and thickly sliced)
14 anchovy fillets (split lengthways, soaked in 2–3 tablespoons milk)
mixed herbs (basil, thyme, sage) – chopped
2 oz Gruyère cheese (grated)

7–8-inch diameter flan ring

This flan, with its black olives and anchovy fillets, is characteristic of dishes from Nice in southern France.

Method

Make the rich shortcrust pastry (see right), line on to the flan ring and chill.

Cook the onions slowly in half the oil for about 20 minutes until golden, and then cool. Stone the black olives.

Spread the mustard over the pastry, place the onions evenly on top, then arrange the tomato slices over and cover these with a lattice of anchovy fillets (well drained from the milk), and place a halved olive in each window pane. Sprinkle a few herbs over the top and finish with the grated cheese. Spoon the remaining oil over flan and bake for about 30–35 minutes in an oven at 400°F or Mark 6.

Rich shortcrust pastry

8 oz plain flour
pinch of salt
6 oz butter
1 egg yolk
2–3 tablespoons cold water

Method

Sift the flour with a pinch of salt into a mixing bowl. Drop in the butter and cut it into the flour until the small pieces are well coated. Then rub them in with the fingertips until the mixture looks like fine breadcrumbs. Mix egg yolk with water, tip into the fat and flour and mix quickly with a palette knife to a firm dough.

Turn on to a floured board and knead lightly until smooth. If possible, chill in refrigerator (wrapped in greaseproof paper, a polythene bag or foil) for 30 minutes before using.

Pipérade

5 eggs
$\frac{3}{4}$ lb ripe tomatoes
2 red peppers, or 2–3 caps of canned pimiento
2 oz butter
1 shallot (finely chopped)
2 cloves of garlic (finely chopped)
salt and pepper
French bread (for croûtes)
little garlic butter

Method

Scald and skin the tomatoes, squeeze to remove seeds and chop flesh roughly. Remove the seeds from peppers and chop, blanch and drain (or chop and drain pimiento).

Melt half the butter in a deep frying pan; put in the tomatoes peppers, shallot and garlic. Season well, cook slowly, stirring occasionally, until it is a rich pulp.

Break eggs into a bowl and beat up with a fork. Cut bread into rounds and spread with a little garlic butter on both sides. Toast until crisp.

Add the remaining butter and eggs to the frying pan and stir with a metal spoon until they start to thicken creamily. Turn into a hot serving dish and surround with the croûtes.

For a picnic, take a small French loaf, cut off the top (lid) and scoop out most of the crumb. Spread inside and out with garlic butter (including the top). Bake in oven at 350°F or Mark 4 until slightly crisp. Fill with the pipérade and replace lid. Cut in slices and serve when cold.

Sole niçoise

2 soles (each weighing $1\frac{1}{4}$ lb – in double fillets)
$2\frac{1}{2}$ fl oz water
squeeze of lemon
slice of onion
salt
6 peppercorns
4 oz long grain rice
3–4 tablespoons French dressing
$7\frac{1}{2}$ fl oz thick mayonnaise
anchovy essence
8 anchovy fillets
$\frac{1}{2}$ lb tomatoes (skinned and sliced)
12 black olives (stoned)

Method

Set oven at 350°F or Mark 4. Poach the fillets in the water, with the lemon juice, onion and seasoning, in pre-set oven for 8–10 minutes. When cooked, take out and leave to cool in the liquor.

Meanwhile cook the rice in plenty of boiling, salted water until tender(about 12 minutes), drain and dry well. Mix the rice with 1 tablespoon of French dressing and add 1–2 tablespoons of the mayonnaise. Place this on a serving dish, drain the fish and arrange it on top of the rice. Season the remaining mayonnaise with anchovy essence to taste and add about $\frac{1}{2}$ tablespoon boiling water if the mayonnaise is still very thick. Coat the fish with the mayonnaise and decorate each fillet with anchovy fillets.

Mix the tomatoes and black olives together with remaining French dressing. Arrange this salad round the fish.

Chiorro

$1\frac{1}{2}$ lb firm white fish (i.e. halibut, turbot, cod, etc. divided into cutlets)
3 tablespoons butter, or oil
4 large onions (thinly sliced)
12 cloves of garlic (very finely chopped)
1 rounded teaspoon tomato purée
1 dessertspoon paprika pepper
pinch of cayenne pepper
pinch of ground mace
salt
black pepper (ground from mill)
2 wineglasses red wine
1 wineglass fish stock, or water
1 tablespoon lemon juice (for poaching the fish)
bread (for croûtes)
oil (for frying)

This is a Basque fish dish and only those who really like garlic should make it.

Method

Heat the butter (or oil) in a shallow saucepan, add the onions and garlic, cover pan and allow them to soften slowly; then remove the lid and increase heat to brown them lightly. Add tomato purée and seasonings, mix well together, then add the wine and stock (or water). Bring sauce to the boil and simmer with the lid off for 10–15 minutes. Adjust seasonings and set sauce aside.

Set oven at 350°F or Mark 4. Wash, dry and trim the fish cutlets. Lay them in a buttered ovenproof dish and season; sprinkle with the lemon juice and poach in pre-set moderate oven for 15–20 minutes. Cut a croûte of bread to fit each cutlet, fry them in oil until golden-brown on both sides. Arrange croûtes in a hot serving dish, set a fish cutlet on each one, then pour a good spoonful of the sauce over each. Serve very hot.

Note: a small quantity of thickening (kneaded butter or arrowroot) can be added.

Whiting alsacienne

4 large whiting fillets ($1\frac{1}{2}$ lb)
1 small firm cabbage
2 oz butter
1 onion (finely sliced)
salt and pepper
1 bayleaf
$2\frac{1}{2}$ fl oz water
1 rounded tablespoon plain flour
$7\frac{1}{2}$ fl oz milk
1 oz dry Cheddar cheese (grated)
1 tablespoon grated Parmesan cheese (to finish)

Method

Cut the cabbage into quarters, removing hard stalk, and shred finely. Melt half the butter in a wide-based flameproof casserole, put in sliced onion; cover, cook for 2–3 minutes, then add the cabbage. Season, cover and cook slowly until soft (15–20 minutes for green cabbage, up to 50 minutes for white).

Fold the fillets, lay in a buttered ovenproof dish, add the bayleaf, seasoning and water. Poach in the oven for about 15 minutes at 350°F or Mark 4.

Melt the rest of the butter in a saucepan, add the flour and strain on the liquor from the fish. Blend sauce until smooth and then stir over gentle heat until thickening slightly. Add the milk, bring to the boil and simmer for 1–2 minutes, remove from the heat and beat in the Cheddar cheese.

Lay the cabbage in a clean ovenproof dish, arrange the fish on the top and spoon over the sauce. Sprinkle with the Parmesan cheese and brown slowly under the grill or in the oven at 400°F or Mark 6.

Cod boulangère

$1\frac{1}{2}$ lb cod steak
2–3 oz butter
3–4 medium-size potatoes
$\frac{1}{2}$ lb button onions
1 teaspoon sugar (for dusting)
squeeze of lemon juice
chopped parsley

Method

Wash and dry cod. Bone steaks and cut into large chunks. Place in an ovenproof dish, melt half the butter and pour over the fish. Cook in the oven at 350°F or Mark 4, basting occasionally, for 15 minutes.

Quarter the potatoes lengthways and trim off the sharp edges. Blanch and drain. Turn them into a frying pan and sauté gently in half the remaining butter until golden-brown. Take out and set aside.

Blanch and drain the onions and fry in the same way in the rest of the butter, adding a dusting of sugar. Cover pan when onions are brown and continue to cook for a few minutes until just tender.

Baste fish once more and surround with the onions and potatoes. Cook in the oven for a further 5 minutes. Squeeze over a little lemon juice and sprinkle well with chopped parsley.

Halibut dieppoise

$1\frac{1}{2}$ lb halibut steak
salt and pepper
juice of $\frac{1}{2}$ lemon
2 oz butter

For salpicon
2 leeks
1 oz butter
1 teaspoon paprika pepper
4 oz prawns (shelled)
black pepper

Halibut dieppoise has a salpicon of prawns and leeks seasoned with paprika and black pepper

Method

Set oven at 350° F or Mark 4. Wash and dry the fish, place it in an ovenproof dish, season and add lemon juice. Melt the 2 oz butter and pour it over the fish; cover and cook in pre-set moderate oven for about 20 minutes. Baste from time to time.

Meanwhile slice the white part of the leeks in rounds, soften in the butter, add the paprika and prawns and heat gently. Shred the green of the leeks and blanch for 2–3 minutes; drain and refresh and add to the pan. Season with black pepper.

Take up the fish carefully, remove the bone and skin and spoon the salpicon over the top.

Pork chops ardennaise

4–5 lean loin pork chops
2 thick gammon rashers (about 8 oz in all)
2 wineglasses white wine
3 shallots (finely chopped)
salt
pepper (ground from mill)
2 tablespoons plain flour
2 oz butter
¼ pint double cream
1 teaspoon French mustard
1 tablespoon chopped parsley

Method

Remove rind from the gammon rashers, cut them into small squares or julienne strips. Place in a bowl and cover with the wine and shallots and leave to soak for about 30 minutes. Then drain gammon and shallots and reserve them and the wine separately. Lightly season the pork chops and roll them in the flour.

Heat the butter over a moderate heat and gently fry the chops for 6–7 minutes on each side. Add the shallots and gammon, continue cooking for 2–3 minutes, then pour on the reserved wine and the cream. Simmer gently for 10–12 minutes.

Take up the chops and arrange them on a hot serving dish. Reduce the sauce a little in the pan, add the French mustard and parsley, taste for seasoning and spoon this sauce over the chops.

Pork chops normande

4 pork chops
1 oz butter
1 oz Parmesan cheese (finely grated)
4 tablespoons double cream
4 tablespoons cider
1 teaspoon white wine vinegar
$\frac{1}{4}$ pint brown stock
1 teaspoon French mustard
salt and pepper

For garnish
2 apples (cored and sliced)
butter (for frying)

Method

Sauté the chops lightly on both sides in the butter. Mix the cheese with 1 tablespoon of cream and spread over the meat. Place in the oven and finish the cooking at 375°F or Mark 5 for 25 minutes.

Take chops out of oven, keep hot. Put cider and vinegar in the pan and boil until reduced to a glaze. Add the stock, remaining cream, French mustard and seasoning to taste. Reheat sauce, but do not boil.

Peel, core and slice apples and fry in butter. Put the chops on a serving dish and pour over the sauce. Garnish with the apple rings.

Serve with sauté potatoes (boil, slice and then fry potatoes in fat until golden-brown).

Ratatouille

$\frac{1}{2}$ lb courgettes
1–2 aubergines
$\frac{1}{2}$ lb, or 1 medium-size can, tomatoes
1 large green pepper
1 large red pepper
2 small onions (finely sliced into rings)
2 cloves of garlic (chopped) – optional
4 tablespoons olive oil
salt and pepper

Method

Slice and salt the courgettes and aubergines and set aside. Scald, skin and remove seeds of fresh tomatoes and slice roughly, or drain canned ones. Halve the peppers, removing core and seeds, and cut into fine shreds.

Heat the oil in a stewpan, and fry the onion rings and garlic for 2–3 minutes. Wipe dry the courgettes and aubergines, add them to the pan and fry for 2–3 minutes on each side, adding extra oil as needed. Season the mixture, add shredded peppers and tomatoes, cover the pan and cook gently for a good hour or more on top of the stove, or in the oven at 350°F or Mark 4. The ratatouille should cook down to a soft, rich mass.

Cold Burgundian ham with parsley

2 lb mild-flavoured cooked ham (thickly sliced)

For wine jelly
$2\frac{1}{2}$ pints chicken, or veal, stock (bouillon cubes will not do)
$\frac{1}{4}$ bottle ($6\frac{1}{4}$ fl oz) white Burgundy, preferably Mâcon
1 dessertspoon tarragon, or white wine, vinegar
2 egg whites
2 large tablespoons chopped parsley

Glass bowl

In Burgundy this dish of ham in white wine jelly is traditionally served on Easter Sunday. It can be prepared the day before it is required.

Method

To make wine jelly: first make sure stock is quite free from grease, well-seasoned and set to a firm jelly. Put it into a large pan with the wine and vinegar and place this over a gentle heat to melt it.

Beat egg whites until frothy, add to pan and whisk down into the stock and wine until mixture begins to boil. Allow to boil undisturbed to the top of pan, then lift carefully away from heat and leave a few minutes until the contents subside.

Boil again twice more, leave to stand for 5 minutes, then strain through a scalded cloth and leave to cool. Cut ham neatly into 2-inch strips and put at the bottom of glass bowl. Press down lightly and continue filling until the bowl is half-full. Moisten ham with the cool jelly and then leave to set.

Watchpoint As cooked ham soon loses its attractive pink colour if left exposed to the air, don't prepare strips until wine jelly has been made and become cool (or cover ham strips with damp greaseproof paper).

Add the parsley to remaining jelly, and when on point of setting pour carefully into the half-full bowl of ham. Leave several hours in a cool place before serving.

Loin of lamb bretonne

2–3 lb loin of lamb (boned)
2–3 tablespoons dripping

For stuffing
2 tablespoons chopped onion
1 oz butter
5 tablespoons fresh white breadcrumbs
2 tablespoons chopped mixed herbs
grated rind and little juice of 1 orange
salt and pepper
beaten egg
seasoned flour
browned breadcrumbs

For sauce
1 onion (sliced)
plain flour
$\frac{1}{2}$ pint stock (made with the bones, 1 onion, 1 carrot and bouquet garni to flavour)
1–2 tablespoons redcurrant jelly
orange juice
12 glazed onions and several carrots (to garnish)

Method

If not boned, ask the butcher to chine the loin, rather than chop it. Prepare the stuffing: cook the onion in the butter until soft but not coloured. Add it to the white crumbs with the herbs, orange rind and seasoning. Bind with the orange juice and a little beaten egg. Spread this over the inside of the meat, roll up and tie securely with string. Roll in seasoned flour, brush with beaten egg and roll in browned crumbs.

Heat the dripping in a roasting tin and, when smoking, put in the meat, baste and set to roast for $1\frac{1}{4}$–$1\frac{1}{2}$ hours. Prepare a good stock from the bones. When cooked, take up the meat, remove string and keep warm while you prepare the sauce. Tip off fat from the roasting tin, leaving the sediment in the bottom. Add the sliced onion and cook slowly until brown. Dust in a little flour, add the stock and redcurrant jelly, boil up well, season, sharpen with a little orange juice and then strain.

Carve the meat, arrange in a serving dish, garnish with glazed onions and carrots (see page 31). Spoon over a little of the sauce and serve the rest separately.

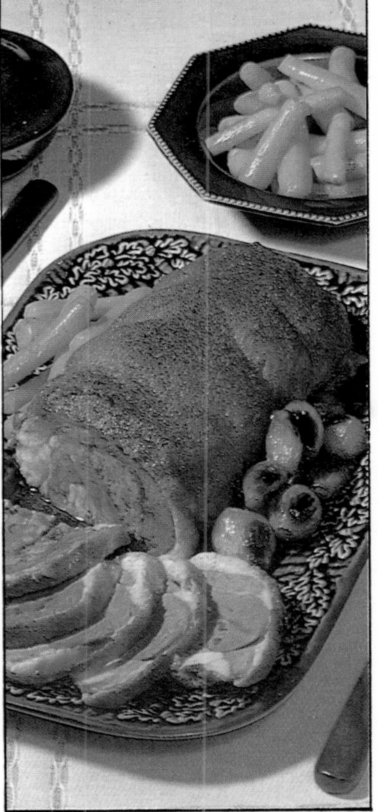

Stuffed pheasant alsacienne

1 plump pheasant
1½–2 oz butter (for roasting)
1 glass sherry
1 wineglass stock
bouquet garni
2–3 sticks of celery, sliced

For farce
1 medium-size onion (finely chopped)
good ½ oz butter
6 oz pork (minced)
2 tablespoons fresh white breadcrumbs
1 teaspoon chopped sage
salt and pepper
1 egg yolk

For sauce
2–3 cooking apples
½ oz butter
salt and pepper
sugar (to taste)
2–3 tablespoons cider
2½ fl oz double cream
1 tablespoon arrowroot (slaked with 2 tablespoons water)

Trussing needle and fine string

This is served with an apple sauce flavoured with cider and with cream added. Also served separately are süsskraut and château potatoes.

Method

Bone out the pheasant, leaving in the leg bones.

To prepare the farce: soften the onion in the butter. Add this to the pork with the bread-crumbs and sage. Season and bind with the egg yolk. Fill the pheasant with this stuffing, re-shape, sew up and truss. Brown carefully in hot butter in a flame-proof casserole, then flame with the sherry. Add stock, bouquet garni and sliced celery. Cover tightly and simmer on low heat or in the oven at 350°F or Mark 4 for 45–50 minutes.

Meanwhile prepare the sauce. Slice the apples without peeling them and cook to a pulp with the butter. Rub through a strainer and return to the pan. Season and add sugar to taste, then pour on the cider. Simmer for 5 minutes.

Take up, carve and dish up the pheasant. Strain the gravy, add to the sauce with the cream and thicken it slightly with a little slaked arrowroot. Spoon some over pheasant; serve rest separately.

Süsskraut

1 small Dutch cabbage
1–2 oz butter
2 tablespoons wine vinegar
1 tablespoon caster sugar
salt and pepper
1 tablespoon chopped parsley

The Alsace region has in the past changed hands many times between France and Germany. Although now thoroughly French, many German words survive locally, hence the name of this dish.

Method

Wash and shred cabbage finely. Well rub a thick pan with butter and pack in the cabbage, adding the vinegar, sugar and seasoning. Cover with buttered paper and the pan lid and cook slowly for 20–25 minutes until the cabbage is just tender. Fork in chopped parsley just before serving.

Glazed carrots

1–2 lb carrots
1 teaspoon sugar
1 oz butter
salt
mint (chopped)

Method

Peel carrots, leave whole, or quarter if small. If very large, cut in thin slices. Put in a pan with water to cover, sugar, butter and a pinch of salt. Cover and cook steadily until tender, then remove lid and cook until all the water has evaporated when the butter and sugar will form a glaze round the carrots.

Add a little chopped mint just before serving.

Glazed onions

Cover 12 button onions with cold water, add salt and bring to the boil. Tip off the water, add 1–1½ oz butter and a dusting of caster sugar. Cover and cook gently until golden-brown on all sides, and cooked through (about 10 minutes).

Le poirat (Pear tart)

2–3 William pears
1 tablespoon water
caster sugar (for dusting)
2½ fl oz double cream (lightly whipped)

For pastry
8 oz plain flour
2 teaspoons ground cinnamon
2 oz shelled walnut kernels (finely chopped)
5 oz butter
4 oz caster sugar
2–3 drops of vanilla essence
1 egg

Deep 7–8 inch diameter flan ring

This is a speciality of the French province of Normandy, which is famed for its excellent fruit and cream.

Method

Sieve the flour with the cinnamon on to a board and mix in the chopped nuts. Make a well in the centre and in it place the butter, sugar, vanilla and egg. Using the fingertips of one hand only, pinch and work the wet ingredients together until well blended. Then draw in the flour and knead lightly until smooth. Set aside in a cool place for about an hour.

Peel, core and quarter pears. Take two-thirds of the pastry, roll it out and line the flan ring. Roll out the remaining pastry and form a round to cover the top; cut a round about 2½ inches in diameter out of the centre of this. Fill the tart with the pears, cover with the pastry ring, brush with water and dust with sugar. Bake in oven preset to 375–400°F or Mark 5–6, for 30–40 minutes.

Serve warm or cold. Just before serving, pour the whipped cream into the centre.

Placing peeled and quartered pears in tart with pointed ends in centre

Placing the ring of pastry on the tart with the aid of a rolling pin

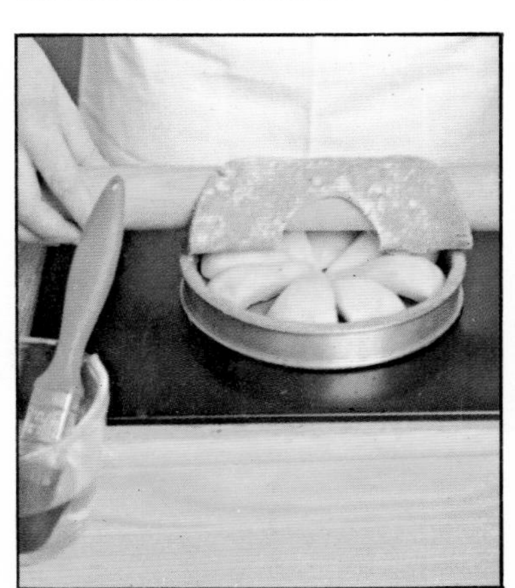

Le poirat, made with cinnamon-flavoured pastry, is served with whipped cream

Gâteau basque

For rich shortcrust pastry
6 oz plain flour
pinch of salt
1 oz shortening
3 oz butter
3 rounded dessertspoons ground almonds
6 dessertspoons caster sugar
1 egg yolk
2–3 drops of vanilla essence
2–3 tablespoons cold water
4–5 heaped tablespoons jam (preferably plum, gooseberry, damson, etc.)
1 egg white (lightly beaten)
caster sugar (for dusting)

6-7 inch diameter flan ring

Method

Rub the fats into the flour and salt, in a bowl, add ground almonds and sugar. Mix egg yolk with vanilla and water in a basin and add to dry ingredients. Work up lightly to a firm paste and chill slightly.

Roll out two-thirds of the dough to $\frac{1}{4}$-$\frac{1}{2}$ inch thickness and line on to the flan ring. Fill with the jam, roll out the rest of the dough to a round and lay over the top. Press down the edges, mark the surface, cart-wheel-fashion, with the point of a knife. Bake for 30–35 minutes in an oven pre-set at 400°F or Mark 6. Lower oven temperature to 375°F or Mark 5 after the first 15 minutes.

When cooked brush the top with lightly beaten egg white, dust with caster sugar and return to oven for 2 minutes to frost the top. Serve hot or cold.

Watchpoint The sugar must be dusted on to the egg white quickly so that they can combine to make a frost topping before the heat of the pastry sets the egg white.

Galette normande

For Danish shortcrust pastry
8 oz plain flour
6 oz butter
$2\frac{1}{2}$ oz icing sugar
2 egg yolks
2–3 drops of vanilla essence

For apple marmelade
$2\frac{1}{2}$ lb cooking apples
$\frac{1}{2}$ oz butter
grated rind of $\frac{1}{2}$ lemon
4–6 oz granulated sugar

For icing
4 rounded tablespoons icing sugar (sifted)
2–3 tablespoons sugar syrup
1–2 drops of vanilla essence
2 tablespoons redcurrant jelly (well beaten)

Paper forcing bag

Method

First prepare Danish shortcrust pastry : sift flour on to your work surface, make a well in the centre and put in the butter, icing sugar, egg yolks and vanilla essence. Work mixture to a smooth paste with your hand, then chill for at least 1 hour before using.

Meanwhile prepare apple marmelade. Wipe, quarter and core the apples ; slice them into a pan, rubbed around with butter, then cover with well-buttered paper and a lid, and cook apples gently to a pulp. Rub this pulp through a fine sieve, then return the purée to the pan with the lemon rind and sugar. Boil rapidly until marmelade is really thick, stirring frequently ; turn it into a flat dish to cool.

Divide the pastry into three, roll out each piece into a round,

8 inches in diameter. Slide these on to baking sheets, prick pastry with a fork and bake in the oven, pre-set at 375°F or Mark 5, for 10–12 minutes, or until a pale, biscuit colour. Leave rounds to cool.

Sandwich the rounds together with apple marmelade. Mix the icing sugar with the sugar syrup and vanilla essence until it is a thick cream. Heat this gently, then coat the galette. Decorate at once with redcurrant jelly, using the paper forcing bag to pipe it in lines on to the cake. Then draw the point of a knife across the jelly lines in alternate directions to 'feather' decoration.

After piping the redcurrant jelly on to the icing, feather the surface using the point of a knife

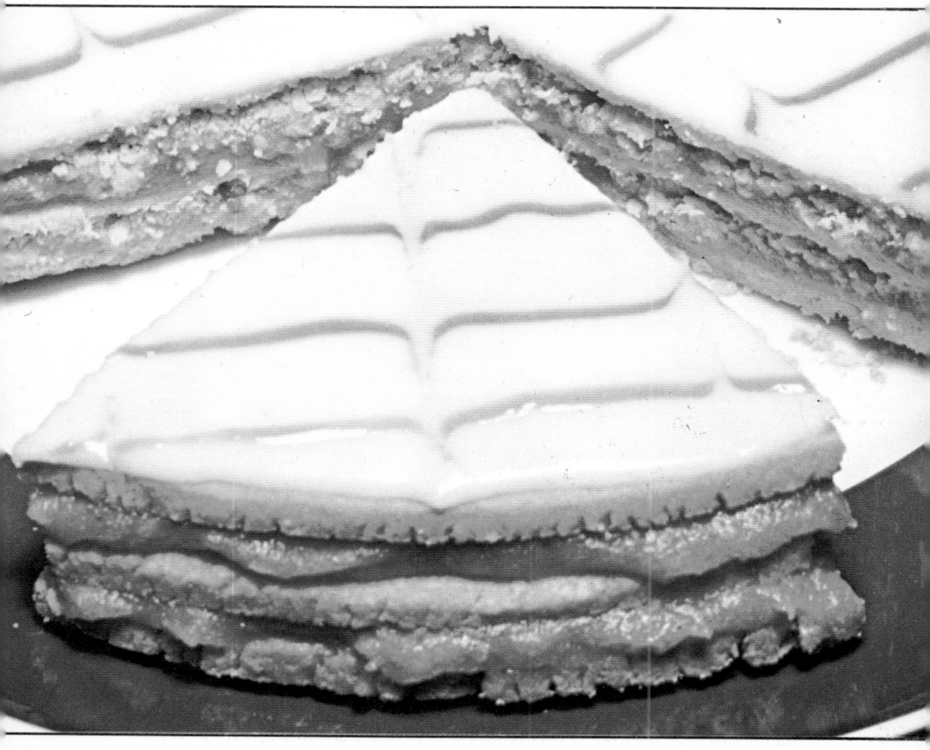

Sauerbraten (Hot spiced beef)

$3\frac{1}{2}$–4 lb top rump, or silverside, or top side, of beef
dripping, or oil and butter
plain flour
$\frac{1}{4}$ pint soured cream (optional)

For marinade
1 tablespoon dry mustard
$\frac{1}{4}$ pint red wine vinegar
$\frac{1}{4}$ pint red wine
$\frac{1}{2}$ pint water
1 medium-size carrot (sliced)
1 medium-size onion (sliced)
2 tablespoons soft brown sugar
2 cloves
1 bayleaf
6 peppercorns
1 teaspoon dried thyme

If you wish to omit the red wine, use $7\frac{1}{2}$ fl oz vinegar and $12\frac{1}{2}$ fl oz water.

Method

Mix the mustard with a little of the vinegar, then put into a pan with the rest of the ingredients for the marinade. Stir until boiling, then pour off and cool. Put the beef into a deep dish and pour over the cold marinade. Cover and leave, preferably in a refrigerator, for 2–3 days, turning the meat occasionally. When ready to cook, take out the beef and wipe it with absorbent paper.

Set the oven at 325°F or Mark 3. Heat the dripping (or oil and butter) in a flameproof casserole and brown the meat all over. Pour over the marinade, bring up to boiling point, cook in pre-set oven for $2\frac{1}{2}$–3 hours

Hot, spiced beef, marinated in red wine, with potato dumplings

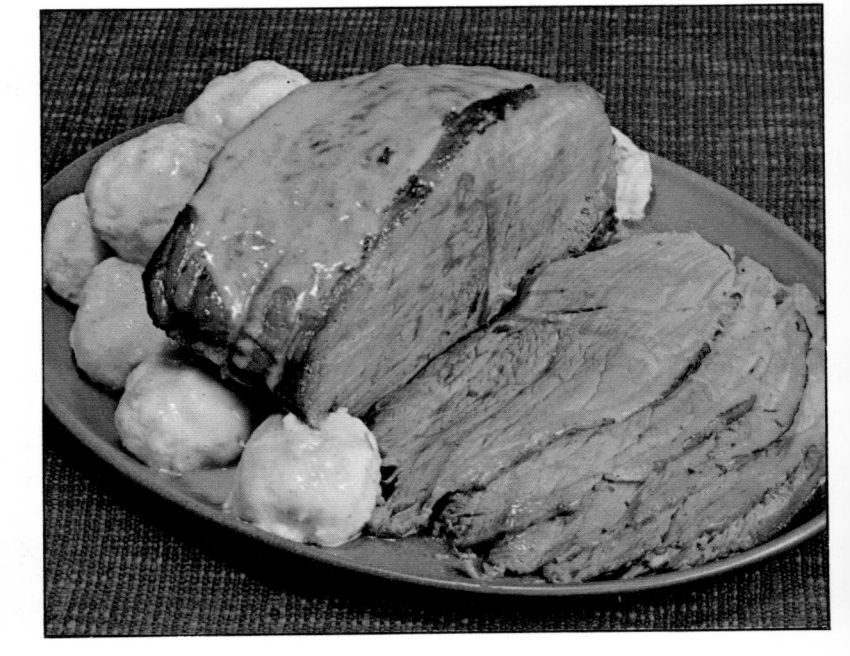

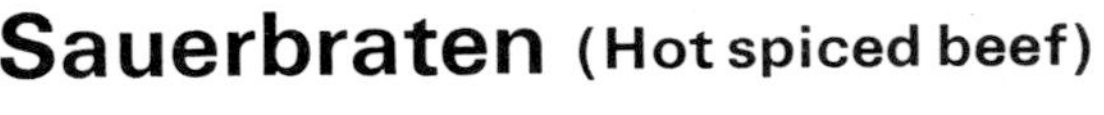

or until tender.

When cooked, take up the meat and strain and measure the liquid. Take a scant 1 oz of flour for each $\frac{1}{2}$ pint of liquid. Slake this flour with a little liquid, then add to the pan and bring to the boil. Beat in the soured cream and adjust the seasoning. Put a little sauce over the joint and pass the rest separately. Serve with potato dumplings.

Potato dumplings

$1\frac{1}{2}$ lb potatoes
1 slice of bread (crust removed)
$\frac{1}{2}$–1 oz butter
good pinch of ground mace
1 small egg
2 oz plain flour
$\frac{1}{2}$ oz cornflour
salt and pepper
melted butter (for serving)

Method

Scrub potatoes and boil in their skins until really tender. Drain and peel, then put through a sieve or mash well. Leave until cold. Meanwhile cut the bread into large dice and fry in the butter until brown. Now add the mace, egg and 2 kinds of flour to the potato and season. Mix well and shape into balls the size of a golf ball. Press 2 pieces of the fried bread into the middle of each dumpling, making sure that the potato covers the bread well.

Have ready a large pan full of boiling salted water and slip the dumplings into the water, being sure not to fill the pan too full – there should be only one layer. Boil gently with the lid off the pan for 12–15 minutes, turning the dumplings occasionally, then drain them well and serve hot with a little melted butter poured over the top.

Salt pork with sauerkraut and frankfurters

1½ lb salt belly of pork
2 oz butter
1½ lb sauerkraut (fresh or canned)
1 medium-size onion (stuck with a clove)
1 carrot (peeled)
2–3 tablespoons dry white wine, or stock, or water
salt and pepper
little kneaded butter

For garnish
2 pairs of frankfurter sausages (poached)
boiled potatoes

Method

Put pork in a large pan, cover with cold water, bring slowly to the boil, simmer gently for about 1 hour, and leave to cool in the liquid. Well grease an ovenproof casserole with half of the butter, arrange the sauerkraut in this with the onion and carrot. Put the pork in the centre, moisten with the wine or stock, or water, season, and cover with buttered paper.

Cover the pan with a tightly fitting lid and cook in oven at 350°F or Mark 4 for about 1½ hours. At end of cooking time liquid should have evaporated.

Take out the pork, bind the sauerkraut with a little kneaded butter, reheat, stirring constantly and add remaining butter.

Slice the pork and serve on the sauerkraut, garnished with the cooked frankfurters and boiled potatoes. The onion and carrot may be sliced and mixed with the sauerkraut if wished.

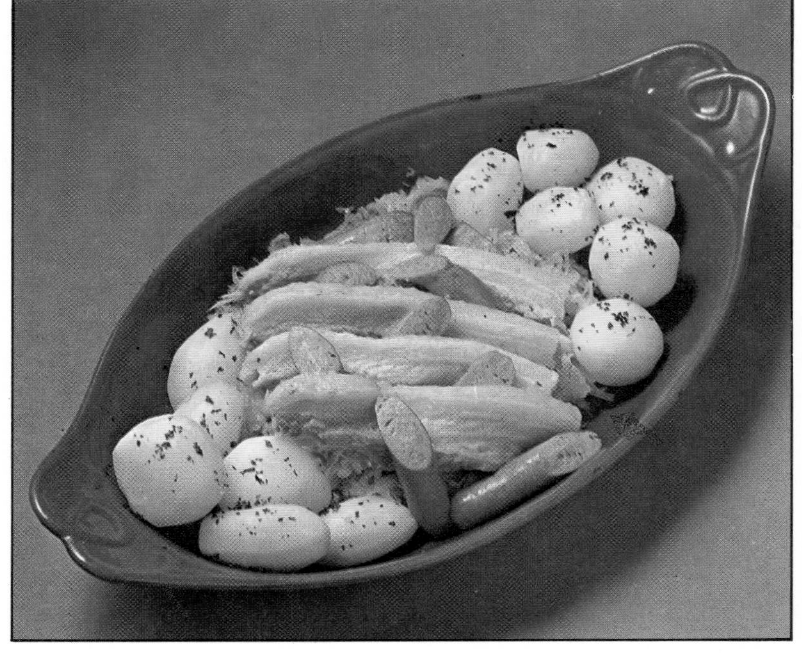

Streusel kuchen

1 quantity of foundation dough (see below)

For streusel
$2\frac{1}{2}$ oz brown sugar
$\frac{3}{4}$ oz plain flour
1 teaspoon cinnamon
1 oz butter (melted)
2 oz walnuts (chopped)

2 lb cake, or loaf, tin

Method

Grease the tin well. Set the oven at 400°F or Mark 6. After the second rising divide the dough into two. Put half into the prepared tin and push it down with your fist. Mix the ingredients for the streusel together, put half of this on top of the dough, then cover with the other half of the dough, and scatter the rest of the streusel mixture over the top.

Prove for 10–15 minutes, then bake for about 45–50 minutes. Test with a thin skewer before taking it out of the oven.

Foundation dough

1 lb plain flour
large pinch of salt
7 fl oz milk
1 oz yeast
4 oz butter
4 oz caster sugar
2 eggs (beaten)

Method

Sift the flour with the salt into a mixing bowl. Warm the milk carefully to blood heat, add to the yeast and butter, stir until dissolved and then mix in the sugar and beaten eggs. Make a well in the centre of the flour, pour in the liquid ingredients and mix until smooth, first with a wooden spoon and then with your hand. When the dough comes away cleanly from the sides of the bowl, turn it on to a floured board and knead until it becomes elastic. Place the dough in a greased bowl (turn it in the bowl so that it is lightly greased all over), cover with a damp cloth and set the dough in a warm place to rise for 45–50 minutes, or until it has doubled in bulk.

Knock down the dough, pull sides to the centre, turn it over, cover and let it rise again for 30 minutes before shaping and baking it. Add fruit when indicated in recipe.

If the dough is not for immediate use, omit the last rising, ie. 30 minutes. Merely knock down the dough, pull sides to centre and turn it over. Cover the top of the basin with a large plate or lid and put into the refrigerator. Keep like this overnight, or longer if wished. Once the dough comes to the top of the bowl, push it down again. When wanted for use take out of the bowl and leave at room temperature for at least 1 hour, by which time the dough should start to rise. At this stage, the filling is added.

The shaping, proving and baking should now take place.

Bavarian apple tart

For rich shortcrust pastry
6 oz plain flour
pinch of salt
4 oz butter
$1\frac{1}{2}$ rounded tablespoons caster sugar
1 egg yolk
3–4 tablespoons milk
icing sugar (for dusting)

For apple mixture
1–$1\frac{1}{2}$ lb cooking apples
1 rounded tablespoon currants
1 rounded tablespoon sultanas
2 tablespoons fresh breadcrumbs
1–2 tablespoons sugar (brown, or white)
1 teaspoon ground cinnamon

Method

Sieve flour and salt into a bowl, lightly rub in the butter, add sugar, mix the egg yolk with the milk and stir in to bind the rich shortcrust pastry together. Set aside to chill.

Now peel, core and slice the apples. Put them into a bowl with the cleaned, dried fruit, crumbs, sugar and cinnamon, and mix well.

Knead pastry lightly to work out any cracks, and roll out thinly to a rectangle about 9 inches by 6 inches. Slide on to a baking sheet (preferably one without edges which makes it easier to remove the tart after cooking). Trim the pastry edges, then place the apple mixture down the middle, leaving about $1\frac{1}{2}$–2 inches of pastry on each side. Lift these sides up and over with a palette knife, so that they rest on the mixture, but leave a gap in the middle to show the filling. Press the pastry down lightly with the knife so that the sides remain in place while baking.

Bake for 35–40 minutes in an oven pre-set at 375°F or Mark 5. Slide on to a rack to cool, then dust thickly with icing sugar before cutting into slices for serving.

Serve with cream or custard separately, or a mixture of thick custard and yoghourt whisked together. Do this when the custard is cold and well sweetened, adding the yoghourt to taste.

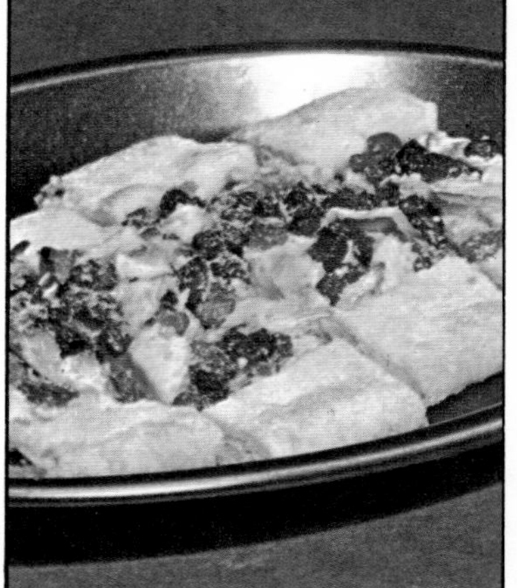

Kugelhopf

about 7 fl oz milk
scant 1 oz yeast
12 oz plain flour
pinch of salt
1 oz caster sugar
2 large, or 3 small, eggs (well broken with a fork)
4 oz butter (melted)
2 oz currants (washed and dried)
2 oz raisins, or sultanas (washed and dried)
about 24 almonds (blanched)
icing sugar (optional)

7–8-inch diameter kugelhopf tin

A kugelhopf is generally eaten with coffee, but not tea. It is baked in a special fluted tin with a tube in the centre, known as a kugelhopf tin.

Method

Butter the tin well. Warm the milk to blood heat, pour on to the yeast and stir until dissolved. Sift the flour and salt into a warm bowl, make a well in the centre, pour in the warm milk and yeast, add the sugar and eggs and the melted (but not hot) butter. Mix thoroughly together, then add the cleaned, dried fruit. Press the blanched almonds round the sides and bottom of the buttered tin. Turn the dough into it so that it is three-quarters full, then stand it in a warm place for about 20–30 minutes, or until the mixture is about 1 inch below the top of the tin.

Meanwhile set the oven at 375–400 °F or Mark 5–6. Stand the tin on a thick baking sheet, then put into the centre of the pre-set oven and bake for 50–60 minutes. If the top tends to colour too much, lower the heat until the kugelhopf is done. Leave for a few minutes before turning out and dust with icing sugar if wanted.

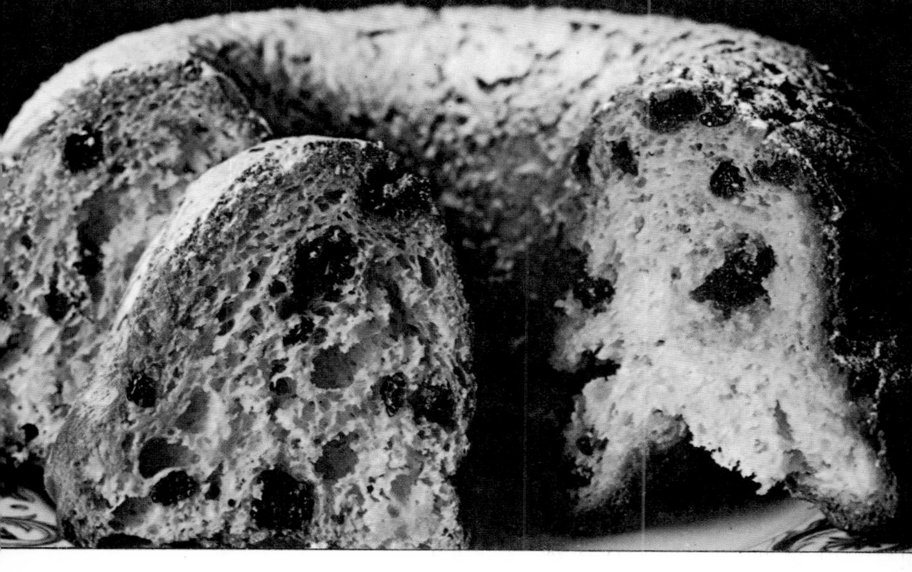

Linzer torte

8 oz plain flour
4 oz butter
4 oz caster sugar
1 whole egg
1 egg yolk
$2\frac{1}{2}$ oz almonds (ground without blanching)

To flavour
pinch of salt
cinnamon
grated lemon rind

For filling
1 lb fresh raspberries
sugar (to sweeten)

To finish
redcurrant, or raspberry, glaze

7-inch diameter flan ring

Method

Bring the raspberries to the boil and cook rapidly for 2–3 minutes with sugar to sweeten.

Sift the flour with salt and cinnamon and make a well in the centre. Place the butter, sugar, eggs and lemon rind in this well and sprinkle almonds on the flour. Work these ingredients together into a dough and leave this in a cool place for 1 hour.

Set the oven at 375°F or Mark 5. Roll out the dough to a thickness of about $\frac{1}{4}$–$\frac{1}{2}$ inch, line into the flan ring and fill with the cold raspberry mixture. Put a lattice of pastry across the top and bake in pre-set oven for 20–30 minutes. When the torte has cooled, brush it with redcurrant (or raspberry) glaze.

1

2

1 *Filling the flan for Linzer torte with cooked raspberries*
2 *Putting a pastry lattice on flan*

Linzer torte, a luscious raspberry flan with lattice pastry and a redcurrant glaze, should be served cold as a dessert or tea-time gâteau

Mohrenköpfe

$2\frac{1}{4}$ oz plain flour
pinch of salt
3 eggs
3 oz caster sugar
caster sugar (for dredging)
chocolate glacé icing, or chocolate marquise
$\frac{1}{4}$ pint Chantilly cream

Forcing bag, $\frac{5}{8}$-inch diameter plain pipe

Mohrenköpfe means literally Moors' heads; these cakes take this name because they are domed and covered with chocolate icing or marquise. This quantity makes about 9 cakes.

Method

Grease and flour a baking sheet; set the oven at 350–375°F or Mark 4–5.

Sift the flour with the salt, whisk the eggs and sugar together over gentle heat until the mixture is thick and mousse-like. Remove the bowl from the heat and continue whisking until it is cold. Using a metal spoon, fold the flour into the mixture with great care. Turn the mixture into the forcing bag fitted with the plain pipe and pipe out drops, 2 inches in diameter, on to the baking sheet.

Dredge cakes lightly with sugar and bake in pre-set moderate oven for about 10 minutes. Allow them to cool, scoop out the centre from the bottom of each one and arrange them, dome side up, on a wire rack ready for icing. Coat with icing (or marquise) and when set, fill each cake with Chantilly cream, then sandwich them together in pairs.

Glacé icing

4-6 tablespoons granulated sugar
$\frac{1}{4}$ pint water
8-12 oz icing sugar (finely sifted)
flavouring essence and colouring (as required)

Method

Make sugar syrup by dissolving granulated sugar in $\frac{1}{4}$ pint of water in a small saucepan. Bring to the boil, and boil steadily for 10 minutes. Remove pan from heat and when quite cold add the icing sugar, 1 tablespoon at a time, and beat thoroughly with a wooden spatula. The icing should coat the back of a spoon and look very glossy. Add flavouring and colouring (if used). Warm the pan gently on a very low heat.

Watchpoint The pan must not get too hot. You should be able to touch the bottom with the palm of your hand.

Spread over cake with a palette knife.

Chocolate marquise

Melt 6 oz plain block chocolate in 2–3 tablespoons water, taking care not to let it get more than lukewarm. Then stir in $\frac{1}{2}$ oz butter or $\frac{1}{2}$ teaspoon oil. Use at once while it is still of a coating consistency.

Minestrone

2 large tablespoons white haricot beans (soaked overnight)
2–3 pints brown stock
2 medium-size carrots
2–3 sticks of celery
1 large onion
2–3 tablespoons oil
2 leeks
2 rashers of fat bacon
1–2 cloves of garlic
$\frac{1}{4}$ of a small cabbage
1 small can tomatoes, or 1 rounded dessertspoon tomato purée
bouquet garni
salt and pepper
Parmesan cheese (grated)

Method

Soak beans overnight then drain, put in a pan with about 1 pint of stock, bring slowly to the boil and simmer for at least 30 minutes. Meanwhile dice the carrots and slice the celery and onion. Heat oil in a stew-pan, put in the prepared vegetables and fry gently for about 5 minutes.

Slice the leeks and cut bacon into small pieces. Crush garlic and shred cabbage.

Pour rest of the stock into the pan and bring to the boil; add sliced leeks, bacon, garlic, tomatoes, or purée, and the bouquet garni. Season and add the beans with their stock. Simmer gently for 30 minutes, then add the shredded cabbage. Cook gently until the vegetables are thoroughly cooked and soup is of a good flavour.

A bowl of grated Parmesan should be served separately.

Italian mussel soup

1 quart mussels
4 tablespoons salad oil
1 clove of garlic (finely chopped)
1 medium-size onion (sliced)
1 medium-size can tomatoes (15 oz)
salt and pepper
$1\frac{1}{4}$ pints fish stock, or water
2 wineglasses white wine
bouquet garni (containing 2 sticks of celery and a strip of lemon rind)
2 rounded tablespoons fresh breadcrumbs
1 tablespoon chopped parsley

Method

Heat the oil, add the garlic and onion and cook gently until they are golden-brown. Tip in the tomatoes and bruise well with a wooden spoon; season lightly, pour on the stock (or water) and bring to the boil. Simmer for 15–20 minutes until reduced and pulpy.

Meanwhile scrub and wash the mussels (see page 153), put in a pan with the wine and bouquet garni. Cook over a steady heat until the mussel shells open, then remove from the heat. Strain off the liquor through muslin and add it to the soup with the breadcrumbs and simmer for 5 minutes. Shell the mussels, discarding the beards, and add them to the soup. Simmer for 5 minutes. Add the parsley and serve.

Minestra

- 1 carrot
- 1 onion
- 2 sticks of celery
- 2 tablespoons oil
- about $2\frac{1}{4}$ pints water
- $\frac{1}{2}$ bayleaf
- 1 small leek
- 6 French beans, or brussels sprouts
- salt and pepper
- 2 small potatoes
- 1 clove of garlic
- 2 tomatoes
- 1 rounded dessertspoon chopped parsley
- Parmesan cheese (grated)

Method

Cut the carrot, onion and celery into medium-thick julienne strips. Heat the oil in a stewpan, put in the vegetable strips and fry until just turning colour; shake and stir occasionally.

Pour on water, add bayleaf. Cut leek and beans or brussels sprouts into shreds and add to the pan. Season lightly and simmer for 30–40 minutes.

Add potatoes, cut in strips, and simmer for a further 20 minutes. Crush garlic with a little salt. Scald tomatoes and skin, cut in quarters, flick out the seeds and cut flesh into strips or chop roughly. Add to the soup with the garlic and parsley. Simmer for a further 10 minutes, adjust seasoning and serve sprinkled with grated cheese.

Add more water during early stages if the soup seems too thick.

Watchpoint To cut an onion into strips, cut in half down from crown to root. Lay onion, cut side downwards, on the board, slice fairly thinly, lengthways. The root, which holds the slices in place, can be trimmed off.

How to cook pasta

Pasta is an Italian word meaning literally a paste of flour and water. Spaghetti, macaroni and other different shapes made of semolina, or flour, water and sometimes eggs, are all pasta. Usually pasta is served with a sauce either mixed in with it, or as an accompaniment. The preliminary cooking is always the same – gentle simmering in salted water or stock until barely tender (10–20 minutes). To test, try a piece between your teeth; it should be just firm (or if you can sever it with your thumb nail it is done). Strain off at once and rinse with 1–2 cups of hot water. Tip back into the saucepan and the pasta is then ready to use. To prevent it becoming sticky if it has to be kept for a little while before finishing off, pour hot water into the pan just to cover the bottom before putting back the pasta; cover pan and leave in a warm place. Just before serving the pasta, toss it with a nut of butter.

Macaroni

These are long tubes about three-eighths of an inch in diameter. Though macaroni can be bought in short lengths it, like spaghetti, is better if left whole or broken in half and lowered gently into the boiling salted water. On contact with the water the tubes will soften and curl easily round the pan.

Spaghetti

In Italian shops or in delicatessens spaghetti can be bought in various grades, ie. degrees of thickness. Naturally the thicker the spaghetti is the longer it will take to cook. Very thin spaghetti is known as vermicelli. This, though it can make a dish on its own, is really best added to a broth, or crushed and used as a coating for a rissole.

Cook spaghetti in the same way as macaroni, but allow 12–15 minutes cooking time. Spaghetti should be slightly firmer than macaroni and though this is largely a question of personal taste it ought not to be soft and pulpy in texture when cooked. Once drained it is returned to the pan with 1 tablespoon of oil, or $\frac{1}{2}$ oz butter and seasoned with salt and pepper ground from the mill. It is then ready to be mixed with the chosen sauce or served plain, with the sauce spooned over the top.

Tagliatelle

This is the ribbon pasta, also called 'nouilles' or noodles. It can be bought in varying widths though the most usual is about $\frac{1}{4}$ inch wide. Tagliatelle is also sold flavoured and coloured with spinach or tomato. Cook as for other pastas, allowing 10–12 minutes boiling time until slightly firm, like spaghetti.

Serve with bolognese, milanese or napolitana sauces and grated Parmesan cheese separately.

Tomato sauce
(For pasta 'al sugo')

1 lb tomatoes, or 1 medium-size can
1 small onion (sliced)
1 oz butter, or 2 tablespoons oil
1 clove of garlic (chopped)
good pinch of dried mixed herbs
1 wineglass brown stock, or water
salt and pepper
tomato purée
½ oz butter

This sauce, which is almost a purée, is made without any thickening, but so reduced that it is red-brown in colour and on the point of 'breaking' (curdling). It is this reduction which gives it its characteristic strong and piquant flavour. This sauce goes very well with spaghetti.

Method

Wipe tomatoes, cut in half and squeeze out seeds. Slice and put into a pan with the onion, butter and garlic. Add herbs and stock or water, season well, cover and cook to a pulp. Rub through a strainer, return to the rinsed out pan and add a little tomato purée to strengthen the flavour. Use your own judgment as to the amount, as this depends on the ripeness of the tomatoes. Add butter and boil until thick, stirring frequently.

When tomatoes are plentiful a double quantity can be made (or more) as it will keep for about a week in a covered container in the refrigerator, or can be deep frozen.

Bolognese sauce

2–3 tablespoons oil
1 medium-size onion (chopped)
2 oz mushrooms (sliced)
¼ lb raw beef (finely minced)
1 rounded dessertspoon tomato purée
pinch of dried oregano
1 clove of garlic (crushed with salt)
¼ of a green pepper (chopped) – optional
7½ fl oz brown stock
salt and pepper

Method

Soften onion in the oil, add the mushrooms, the mince, purée, oregano, crushed clove of garlic and green pepper if used.

Fry mixture for a few minutes, then stir in the stock. Season, cover and simmer for 25–30 minutes or until meat is tender. If sauce gets too thick add a little more stock. Spoon sauce over cooked spaghetti.

Milanese sauce

4 oz mushrooms (sliced)
$\frac{1}{2}$ oz butter
$\frac{1}{2}$ pint strong, well-flavoured tomato sauce
4 oz lean cooked ham (shredded)
8 oz spaghetti

This sauce is excellent to serve with spaghetti or any type of pasta, especially when served as a main course. In this case extra ham and mushrooms can be added as in this recipe. Otherwise, it is only necessary to use 2 oz each of mushrooms and ham to $\frac{1}{2}$ pint tomato sauce.

Method

Sauté mushrooms in the butter for 3–4 minutes, then add the sauce. Simmer for a few minutes, then add the ham. Have ready the spaghetti cooked, well drained and mixed with $\frac{1}{2}$ oz butter. Add the sauce and toss up over heat. Serve with grated Parmesan cheese.

Napolitana sauce

1 oz butter, or 2 tablespoons oil
1 medium-size onion (thinly sliced)
1 dessertspoon plain flour
1 wineglass brown stock
1 lb ripe tomatoes (skinned, the stalk cut out and the tomatoes lightly squeezed to remove seeds)
1 clove of garlic (crushed with salt)
1 teaspoon tomato conserve, or purée
1 bayleaf
pinch of sugar
salt
pepper (ground from mill)

This tomato sauce is not reduced as much as that in the al sugo recipe, and is rougher in texture. Serve mixed with, or over, pasta, or if preferred the pasta and sauce can all be turned into a gratin dish and browned in the oven.

Method

Melt butter or oil in a shallow saucepan, add onion, fry gently for 3–4 minutes, then stir in flour and add stock. Bring to the boil. Slice tomatoes and add with the garlic, conserve or purée, bayleaf, sugar, salt and pepper.

Simmer for 25–30 minutes or until well reduced to a thick rich pulp. Remove bayleaf. Have the pasta ready, put in a serving dish and spoon the sauce over the top.

Serve with either spaghetti, macaroni or tagliatelle.

Cannelloni

1 packet cannelloni (about $\frac{1}{2}$ lb) – allow 3–4 tubes per person
$\frac{3}{4}$ pint thin tomato sauce
grated Parmesan cheese

For filling
$\frac{1}{2}$ lb raw veal, or pork (minced), or a mixture of both
$\frac{1}{4}$ pint béchamel sauce (made with 1 oz butter, 1 oz flour, $\frac{1}{4}$ pint of milk)
1 egg yolk
salt and pepper
pinch of ground mace, or grated nutmeg

These are fat tubes of pasta about $2\frac{1}{2}$ inches long. They are partially cooked then filled with a mince of chicken or veal or spinach and curd cheese.

Method

First prepare filling. Make the béchamel sauce and leave to get quite cold before adding to the mince. Mix thoroughly, then add yolk and seasoning. The consistency must be quite stiff. Set filling aside.

Simmer the cannelloni in plenty of boiling salted water for about 7 minutes, then lift out carefully, dip into cold water, drain on cloth or absorbent paper.

Put filling into a forcing bag with large, plain pipe, then pipe into the cannelloni. Put them in a well-buttered flameproof casserole and pour over the tomato sauce (this should just cover). Bring to boiling point on top of stove, then cover and cook in the oven at 350°F or Mark 4 for 40–45 minutes. Ten minutes before end of cooking time, take off lid, sprinkle well with the cheese, increase the heat of oven to 375°F or Mark 5 and brown the surface.

If preferred, the cannelloni may be served without browning, just sprinkle well with the cheese before taking to table.

Spinach and curd cheese filling

1 small packet of frozen spinach purée, or $\frac{1}{2}$–$\frac{3}{4}$ lb fresh spinach
2 oz curd, or cream, cheese
salt and pepper
small pinch of ground mace, or grated nutmeg

Method

If using frozen spinach, put into a pan and cook gently, stirring occasionally until firm. If fresh, boil, drain and dry; sieve to a purée or chop very finely. Sieve cheese and mix in the spinach when cold. Season well and add spice. The mixture should be a firm purée.

Savoury meat filling

1 cup cooked chicken, or ham (minced)
2 tablespoons thick béchamel, or tomato, sauce (sufficient to bind the meat)
3 teaspoons chopped mixed herbs, or parsley
1 egg yolk

Method

Mix ingredients together and season well. The mixture must be firm and quite stiff.

Ravioli

This consists of little rounds or squares of pasta filled with a savoury mince or a mixture of spinach and curd cheese (see page 51). Ravioli can be bought in some Italian provision shops or delicatessens freshly made and ready for cooking. Simmer in stock or water for 15–20 minutes, drain and cover ravioli with a good tomato sauce; continue to simmer gently until golden. Serve well dusted with grated cheese.

To make ravioli at home, use the following recipe.

Ravioli paste

10 oz plain flour
½ teaspoon salt
1½ tablespoons olive oil
2 eggs (beaten)
3–4 tablespoons milk, or water

Method

Sift the flour with salt on to a laminated plastic work top or board, make a well in the centre and put in the oil, eggs and half the milk or water.

Start mixing in the oil, eggs and water gradually, drawing in the flour, add the rest of the liquid as it is needed. Continue to work up the paste until it is smooth and firm, knead well, then cover with a cloth and leave for 20–30 minutes to get rid of any elasticity. Cut in half and roll out one piece, paper thin. Slide to one side then roll

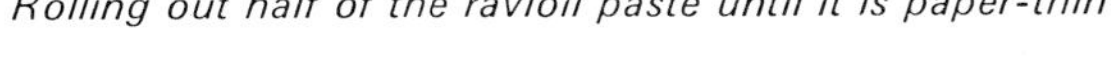
Rolling out half of the ravioli paste until it is paper-thin

out the second piece as thinly, brush with water and put out the chosen filling in teaspoons at regular intervals on the pastry. Lift the first piece on top and with a small ball of the paste press down the top piece around each mound of filling. Stamp out each one with a small fluted cutter or cut out in squares with a pastry wheel. Leave for 2–3 hours to dry a little, then cook as described.

1

2

1 *Spooning cooked spinach and curd cheese filling on to paste*
2 *Cutting filled ravioli into squares with a pastry wheel*

Tortelli

8 oz Ricotta, or curd, cheese
2 oz grated Parmesan cheese
1 egg
1 egg yolk
salt and pepper
pinch of allspice
1 tablespoon chopped parsley
ravioli, or tagliatelle, paste (quantity made with 12 oz flour)
2–3 tablespoons melted butter
1–2 tablespoons grated Parmesan cheese

Method

Mix the cheeses together and beat until smooth, then add the egg and egg yolk, seasonings and parsley. Roll out the dough very thinly, stamp into rounds about $2\frac{1}{2}$ inches in diameter. Put 1 teaspoon of cheese mixture in the centre of each round, brush round the edge with water and fold over like a turnover, press edges down firmly and leave for 30 minutes.

Have ready a large pan of boiling salted water, put in the little turnovers and simmer for 15–20 minutes. Then lift out with a draining spoon, drain well on a cloth or piece of muslin, turn on to a dish, spoon the melted butter over them and dust well with the Parmesan cheese. Serve very hot.

Basic pizza dough

1 lb plain flour
1 teaspoon salt
1 oz yeast
2 teaspoons sugar
about $\frac{1}{4}$ pint milk (warmed)
3–4 eggs (beaten)
4 oz butter (creamed)

Method

Sift the flour and salt into a warmed basin. Cream yeast and sugar and add to the warmed milk with the beaten eggs; add this liquid to the flour and beat thoroughly. Work the creamed butter into the dough. Cover and leave for 40 minutes to rise. **Note**: for the best pizza, it is wise to use a flan ring to keep the dough in position. It has the added advantage of enabling you to cover the entire surface with topping without it running and sticking to your baking sheet.

The name **Pizza** originated from the area around Naples. It is not certain, however, that the nearby village of Pizza, where the flour for the best pizza dough is grown and ground, can claim to be its creator. A pizza may first have been made to use up left-over bread dough and tomato sauce, plus whatever sausage, ham or cheese happened to be available.

Pizza napolitana

$\frac{1}{4}$ quantity of basic dough

For topping
4–6 anchovy fillets
2 tablespoons milk
1 lb ripe tomatoes
1–2 tablespoons olive oil
1 small onion (finely chopped)
1 dessertspoon chopped marjoram, or basil
salt and pepper
4 oz Bel Paese, or Mozzarella, cheese (sliced)

8-inch diameter flan ring

Method

Flour the dough lightly and pat it out with the palm of your hand on floured baking sheet to a round 8 inches in diameter. Then place greased flan ring over it.

Split the anchovy fillets in two lengthways and soak them in the milk; set aside.

Scald and skin the tomatoes, cut away the hard core, squeeze gently to remove seeds, then slice. Heat the oil in a frying pan; add chopped onion and, after a few minutes, the sliced tomatoes. Draw pan aside and add the herbs; season well.

Set oven at 400°F or Mark 6.

Cover dough with tomato mixture, place cheese slices on this and arrange anchovies lattice-wise over the top. Prove pizza for 10–15 minutes, then bake in pre-set oven for 30–35 minutes. Lift off flan ring and slide pizza on to a bread board or wooden platter to serve.

Four different pizzas shown here include three for which recipes are given on these pages

Haddock and mushroom pizza

$\frac{1}{4}$ quantity of basic dough

For topping
1 lb smoked haddock
béchamel sauce (made with 1 oz flour, 1 oz butter, $\frac{1}{4}$ pint flavoured milk)
1 oz butter
1 shallot (finely chopped)
6 oz mushrooms (quartered)
salt and pepper

8-inch diameter flan ring

Method

Cover the smoked haddock with water, bring it slowly to the boil; cover, turn off heat and leave for 10 minutes.

Meanwhile make béchamel sauce in the usual way.

Remove skin and bones from the haddock and flake flesh carefully. Melt 1 oz butter, add shallot, cook for 2–3 minutes, then add quartered mushrooms and sauté briskly for 2–3 minutes. Add béchamel sauce and haddock; season to taste.

Set oven at 400°F or Mark 6. Pat out the dough as before, cover with topping, prove and bake in pre-set hot oven.

Pizza Cordon Bleu

$\frac{1}{4}$ quantity of basic dough

For topping
2 shallots (finely chopped)
1 wineglass white wine
1 lb scampi
4 oz mushrooms (chopped)
1 oz butter
$\frac{3}{4}$ oz plain flour
1 clove of garlic (crushed with $\frac{1}{2}$ teaspoon salt)
$\frac{1}{4}$ pint chicken stock
1 teaspoon tomato purée
4 tomatoes
salt and pepper

8-inch diameter flan ring

Method

Simmer shallot in white wine until reduced to half the quantity. Add scampi and mushrooms and cook very slowly for 5 minutes; set pan aside.

Melt butter, add flour and when coloured add the garlic, stock and tomato purée, stir until boiling, then cook for 3–4 minutes. Scald tomatoes, skin, quarter, and remove seeds, cut flesh again into strips. Add scampi mixture to tomatoes and sauce. Season to taste.

Set oven at 400°F or Mark 6. Pat out the dough as before and cover with the topping; prove and bake in pre-set hot oven.

Cod alla napolitana

2 lb fresh cod
2 tablespoons plain flour
oil (for frying)

For tomato sauce
1 tablespoon oil
2 cloves of garlic (chopped)
$\frac{1}{2}$ lb tomatoes (sliced)
salt and pepper
1 tablespoon capers
12 black olives (stoned)
pinch of cayenne pepper
1 cap of canned pimiento (chopped)

This dish is prepared in Italy with salt cod and served on Good Friday, but in this country fresh cod can be used instead.

Method

Cut the fish from the bone, remove the skin and cut into 2-inch squares. Dust lightly with flour and quickly fry 2–3 pieces at a time until golden-brown in a little hot oil. Drain and put into an ovenproof dish.

Wipe out the pan, add the oil with the chopped garlic and fry gently for a few seconds until golden-brown. Remove the garlic from the oil, add the tomatoes, season and cook until pulpy. Rub through a strainer and return to the pan with the capers, olives, cayenne and pimiento. Simmer for 2–3 minutes. Spoon this sauce over the cod in the dish, cover with a buttered paper and bake in a moderate oven, 350°F or Mark 4, for 15–20 minutes.

Cod alla romana

2 lb fresh cod
salt
2 tablespoons plain flour
oil (for frying fish)
3 green peppers
3–4 tablespoons olive oil
2 onions (sliced)
1 lb tomatoes (scalded, skinned, seeds removed, flesh roughly chopped)
1 tablespoon chopped parsley

This recipe has also been adapted to use fresh, rather than salt, cod.

Method

Cut the fish from the bone, remove the skin and cut flesh into 2-inch pieces. Sprinkle with salt and leave for 30 minutes to draw out the moisture. Tip off any liquid, dry on absorbent paper and roll in a little flour. Fry the fish quickly in a little hot oil until golden-brown, then remove from the pan, drain well and keep on one side.

Cut the green peppers in half, remove the core and seeds and cut flesh into thin strips. Drop the strips into boiling salted water, cook for 1 minute then drain, refresh and drain again. Heat the oil in a large pan, add the onions and cook slowly until golden, then mix in the tomatoes, and cook slowly for about 15 minutes. Then add the green peppers and continue to cook until tender. Add the pieces of fish, simmer for 10 minutes and then serve in a hot dish, sprinkled with the chopped parsley.

Ossi buchi

2 lb shin of veal (cut in slices 2 inches thick)
1 oz butter
1 onion (sliced)
1 carrot (sliced)
1 wineglass white wine
$\frac{1}{2}$ lb tomatoes
1 dessertspoon tomato purée
1 clove of garlic (crushed with $\frac{1}{2}$ teaspoon salt)
$\frac{1}{2}$–$\frac{3}{4}$ pint of jellied bone stock
bouquet garni
salt and pepper
1 tablespoon chopped parsley

Method

Brown the veal in the butter and lift carefully out of the pan. Add the onion and carrot, cover the pan and cook over a steady heat, without stirring, for 2–3 minutes. Put the veal back into the pan, making sure that the bones remain upright so the marrow does not fall out as the meat cooks. Pour over the white wine and allow to reduce to half quantity.

Meanwhile scald and skin the tomatoes, cut away the hard core, squeeze to remove a certain amount of the seeds and chop the flesh finely. Add this to the pan with the tomato purée and cook for 10–15 minutes. Then add the garlic, stock and bouquet garni. Cover the pan and cook for $1\frac{1}{2}$ hours.

Take up the veal and arrange in a serving dish. Tip the contents of the pan into a conical strainer and press well. **Watchpoint** All the tomato pulp should go through the strainer but the carrots and onion should remain behind. Reduce this sauce rapidly until syrupy, adjust the seasoning, spoon over the veal, dust with the chopped parsley and serve with a risotto milanese.

Ossi buchi alla milanese

- 2–2$\frac{1}{2}$ lb knuckle of veal (cut into rounds 1$\frac{1}{2}$–2 inches thick)
- 2 oz butter
- 2 wineglasses white wine
- 1 lb tomatoes
- about $\frac{1}{4}$ pint brown stock
- salt and pepper
- 1 clove of garlic (chopped)
- 3 rounded tablespoons chopped parsley
- grated rind of 1 lemon

Method

Heat a large shallow pan, or flameproof casserole, put in the butter and, when foaming, brown 2–3 slices of veal at a time, taking them out carefully. When all are browned, replace the slices in the pan, but see that the bones remain upright so that the marrow does not fall out during cooking. Pour over the wine, cover and simmer gently for 10–12 minutes.

Meanwhile scald, skin and squeeze the tomatoes to remove any seeds, then chop the flesh. Add this to the pan with the braise in the oven pre-set at 350°F or Mark 4, or on top of the stove on a low heat, for 1–1$\frac{1}{2}$ hours. The veal should be really tender. Mix the garlic with the parsley and the grated lemon rind. Dish up the veal, then sprinkle this parsley mixture on top. This special topping is unique to the Milanese way of cooking ossi buchi and is called 'gremolata'.

Risotto milanese

- 8 oz thick grain rice (preferably Italian)
- 1 marrow bone (optional)
- 2 oz butter
- 1 small onion (finely chopped)
- 1 clove of garlic (chopped, or crushed, with $\frac{1}{2}$ teaspoon salt)
- 1 pinch of saffron (soaked in 2 tablespoons hot water) – optional
- about 1$\frac{1}{4}$ pints chicken, or veal, stock
- salt and pepper
- 2–3 tablespoons Parmesan cheese (grated)

Method

Scoop out marrow from the bone and cut in small pieces. Melt a good half of the butter in a shallow pan or flameproof casserole, add marrow, onion and garlic. Fry gently for 4–5 minutes, add rice and continue to fry, stirring continually until all the grains look white – 4–5 minutes.

Then add saffron in its liquid and about a third of the stock. Season and simmer, stirring occasionally until rice thickens, then add another third of the stock. Continue in this way until the grains are barely tender and the risotto creamy.

Draw pan aside, dot the surface with the remaining butter and sprinkle with 2–3 tablespoons of Parmesan cheese. Cover rice and leave for 5 minutes, or until ready to serve. Stir once or twice with a fork, then turn into a hot dish. Avoid touching with a spoon as this makes it mushy.

Note: bone marrow is characteristic of a risotto milanese but both it and the saffron may be omitted.

Stufato di manzo alla romana
(Beef casserole, Roman-style)

2 lb topside of beef
1 oz butter
1 tablespoon oil
2 onions (chopped)
2 cloves of garlic (crushed)
$\frac{1}{4}$ lb pickled pork (diced)
1 tablespoon plain flour
1 wineglass red wine
$\frac{1}{2}$–$\frac{3}{4}$ pint brown stock
bouquet garni
salt and pepper
4 tomatoes (scalded and skinned)

Method

Set the oven at 350°F or Mark 4. Heat the oil and butter in a large flameproof casserole, put in the beef and brown on all sides; take out and put in the onions, garlic and pork. Fry for about 5 minutes, draw aside, shake in the flour, brown it slightly then pour in the red wine and stock and add the bouquet garni. Season and bring to the boil. Replace the beef, cover the casserole and braise in the pre-set oven for $1\frac{1}{2}$–2 hours, basting well. Quarter the tomatoes and add them to the casserole 30 minutes before the end of the cooking time.

Take up the beef, carve and lay in a deep dish. Skim the gravy, remove the herbs, reduce gravy slightly and spoon over and round beef. Arrange polenta balls at each end of the dish.

Polenta balls

5 tablespoons polenta (maize meal)
$\frac{1}{2}$–$\frac{3}{4}$ pint water
$\frac{1}{2}$ oz butter
1 egg
1 tablespoon grated cheese
salt and pepper
French mustard

For crumbing
1 beaten egg
dry white breadcrumbs

Deep fat bath

Method

Bring the water to the boil, sift in the polenta and simmer for 7 minutes, stirring frequently. Take off the heat and beat in the butter, egg and cheese, then season well with salt, pepper and mustard. Spread on a plate to cool. Shape into small balls on a floured board, brush with beaten egg and roll in breadcrumbs. Fry in deep fat until golden-brown. Serve with stufato di manzo alla romana.

Fritto misto alla milanese

- 2 large escalopes of veal
- 6 oz calves liver (thinly sliced)
- $\frac{1}{2}$ lb lambs sweetbreads
- $\frac{1}{4}$–$\frac{1}{2}$ pint white stock
- 2 sets of calves brains
- 1–2 veal, or lambs, kidneys
- 1 small cauliflower
- 1 small marrow
- 2 baby globe artichokes
- creamed potatoes
- seasoned flour
- 2 eggs (beaten)
- 8–12 oz dried white breadcrumbs
- about 6 oz butter (for frying)
- 1–2 oz butter (for sauce)
- juice of $\frac{1}{2}$ lemon

Method

First prepare all the ingredients before frying, then fry in the order given.

Bat the escalopes out thinly and cut each one into 3 pieces. Roll in seasoned flour.

Roll liver in seasoned flour.

Prepare the sweetbreads and simmer them in stock barely to cover until tender, drain and cool. Roll in flour, coat with egg and crumbs.

Prepare the brains, blanch them, drain, cut in half, roll in flour, coat with egg and ▶

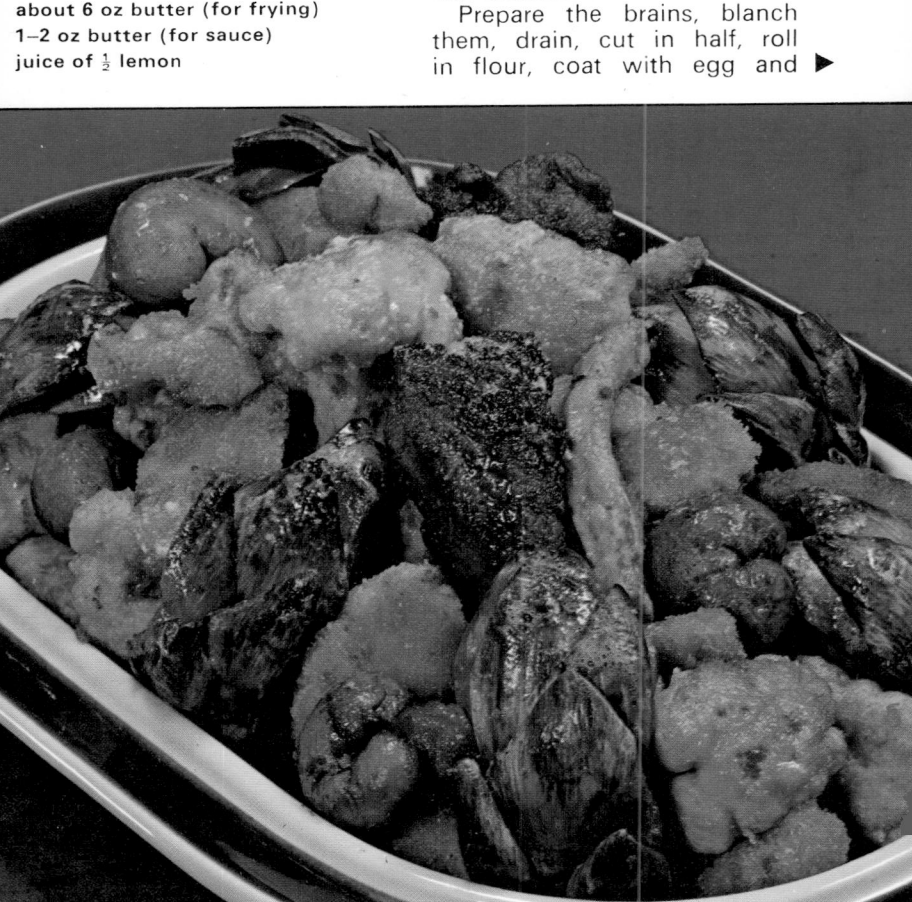

Fritto misto alla milanese continued

breadcrumbs.

Skin and split, or slice, the kidneys.

Break the cauliflower into sprigs, boil and drain it and roll in seasoned flour, then dip in beaten egg.

Slice the marrow, blanch and drain it, then roll in flour and dip in egg.

Boil the artichokes and cut them into quarters.

Divide the creamed potatoes and roll each section into a cork shape. Roll in seasoned flour, dip in beaten egg and roll in breadcrumbs. Use two palette knives to handle the potato croquettes.

Now heat a frying pan, put in some butter and begin to fry the ingredients in the order in which they were prepared, ie. begin with the escalopes and end with the potato croquettes, keeping them warm on a rack.

When all are done, pile up in a dish for serving. Wipe out and reheat the frying pan, drop in the 1–2 oz butter, cook to a nut-brown, add the lemon juice and pour this sauce, foaming, over the fritto misto.

Fritto misto

There are several varieties of this delicious dish, hailing from the different cities: Rome, Florence, Milan. They differ in the amount and type of ingredients in each dish and the way in which they are fried. Flour, egg-and-crumb, and fritter batter are all used as coatings for the various ingredients: meat and offal, vegetables, or fish.

Fritto misto alla fiorentina is similar to the milanese but has not quite so many ingredients. All of the ingredients are egg and crumbed and fried in deep hot oil, as opposed to butter. Typical ingredients are sweetbreads, small lamb cutlets, brains, tiny potato croquettes, sliced courgettes and baby globe artichokes.

Mock scaloppine

$\frac{3}{4}$ lb veal (finely minced)
1 small onion (very finely chopped)
1 clove of garlic (very finely chopped)
1 rounded tablespoon parsley
pinch of dried oregano
salt and pepper
3 eggs
seasoned flour
2–3 oz butter
1 sherry glass Marsala
$\frac{1}{2}$ sherry glass white stock

Method

Put the veal into a basin and add the onion, garlic, parsley and oregano; season well. Beat the eggs with a fork and add to the veal gradually, being careful not to get the mixture too wet. Shape on a wet board into rounded cakes, similar to a fish cake. Leave for $1\frac{1}{2}$–2 hours.

Roll or pat out the cakes into the shape of an escalope with the palm of your hand. Dust well with seasoned flour. Heat a large frying pan, drop in the butter and while still foaming put in the 'escalopes'; cook them gently until nicely brown on each side. Take them out of the pan and dish up, slightly overlapping, down the centre of a hot dish. Add the Marsala and stock to the pan, boil up and spoon over the escalopes. Serve with vegetable salad.

Vegetable salad

1 Spanish onion (finely sliced and separated into rings)
2 cucumbers (peeled and sliced)
1 head of celery (washed and sliced)
salsa verde (see page 64)
1 bunch of radishes

Method

Blanch the onion, then drain, put into fresh cold water, bring once more to the boil and cook for 7–8 minutes, drain and refresh. The onion should be lightly crisp but not too soft. Put the cucumber slices into iced water for 15 minutes, then drain and dry well with absorbent paper or cloth. Arrange the cucumbers, onion and celery in layers, piling them up into a pyramid. Pour salsa verde over the vegetables and garnish with the radishes, sliced or in roses.

Salsa verde (Green sauce)

1 large handful of parsley
1 rounded tablespoon capers
1–2 cloves of garlic
1–2 anchovy fillets
3–5 tablespoons olive oil
1 slice of white bread
1 tablespoon lemon juice
salt and pepper

Method

Pick the parsley from the stalks, chop it, pound or blend with capers, garlic and anchovies. Spoon 1–2 tablespoons of oil over the bread and, when soaked, add to the parsley mixture and continue to pound. Gradually add 2–3 tablespoons of oil; add lemon juice and season well. The sauce should be thick.

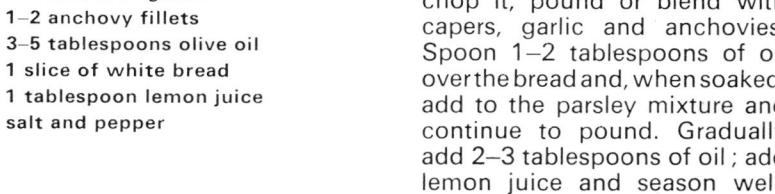

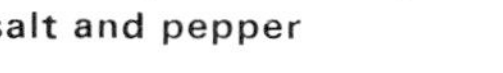

Polpetta alla milanese

1 pork fillet, or tenderloin (weighing about 12 oz)
4 oz minced pork
4 oz sausage meat
1 clove of garlic (crushed with a little salt)
1 teaspoon chopped parsley
1 tablespoon grated Parmesan cheese
black pepper
little grated nutmeg
1 egg (beaten)
about ¼ lb green streaky bacon (cut at No. 4)
1 tablespoon seasoned flour
2 oz clarified butter
1 wineglass white wine

Method

Cut the pork fillet into thin slices and bat out with a rolling pin or a bottle. Mix the minced pork, sausage meat, garlic, parsley, cheese and seasoning together, and add a little beaten egg to bind. Spread out the bacon rashers with a knife blade. Put a layer of the stuffing mixture on to each slice of pork, roll up, wrap in a slice of the bacon and fasten with a cocktail stick. Dust with a little seasoned flour.

Set oven at 350°F or Mark 4. Heat the butter, put in the pork rolls and cook gently until golden-brown all over. Pour over the white wine and allow to reduce to half quantity, then cover the pan tightly and put in the pre-set moderate oven for 30–40 minutes. Serve this with a risotto milanese (see page 59) and a green vegetable.

Bigne di cavalfiore
(Cauliflower fritters)

1 large cauliflower
1 bayleaf
¾ pint thick béchamel sauce (made with 2 oz butter, 2 oz flour and ¾ pint flavoured milk)–cooled
1 bunch of parsley
tomato sauce (for serving)

For fritter batter
¼ pint lukewarm water
1 tablespoon olive oil, or 1 oz butter (melted)
1 egg yolk
1 tablespoon double cream (optional)
4 oz plain flour
½ teaspoon salt
2 egg whites (stiffly whipped)

Deep fat bath

Method

Break the cauliflower into sprigs, using the stalks, and boil with bayleaf in lightly salted water 7–10 minutes, until barely cooked; drain and cool. Stir water, oil (or butter), egg yolk and cream (if used) into the flour and add the salt to make batter. Fold in egg whites just before frying.

Dip each cauliflower sprig into the béchamel sauce, and make sure each is thickly and completely coated. Refrigerate. When really firm, heat deep fat bath to 350–400°F, dip sprigs into batter and then drop carefully into the fat. Fry until a deep golden-brown, then drain on a rack or on crumpled absorbent paper. Fry parsley. Put cauliflower on a napkin in serving dish, garnish with fried parsley and serve tomato sauce separately.

Amaretti secchi
(Dry macaroons)

$3\frac{1}{2}$ oz ground almonds
$4\frac{1}{2}$ oz caster sugar
$1\frac{1}{2}$ oz vanilla sugar
2 egg whites
2 tablespoons kirsch
3–4 almonds (split and shredded)
icing sugar (for dusting)

Method
Set oven at 350°F or Mark 4. Pounds the almonds and both kinds of sugar with 1 egg white. Whip the second egg white until stiff and fold it into the almond mixture with the kirsch. Divide the mixture into pieces the size of a walnut, roll between the palms of your hands and place on a sheet of non-stick cooking paper on a baking sheet and cook in the pre-set oven for 20–30 minutes. Place a shred of almond on the top of each macaroon and dust with a little icing sugar.

Zuppa inglese

$\frac{1}{2}$ pint double cream
4 oz dark chocolate (melted with 1 tablespoon water)
1 packet (12–18) sponge fingers
2 wineglasses sweet white wine
1 oz almonds (blanched and chopped)
1 tablespoon glacé fruits (chopped) – optional

5–6 inch diameter cake tin with loose bottom

Zuppa is Italian for soup, but this recipe for 'English soup' is well known to mean a dessert made from liquor-soaked sponge.

Method
Whip the cream lightly, fold in the cold melted chocolate. Place the sponge fingers in a shallow dish and moisten with the wine. Take the cake tin and cover bottom with a layer of the cool cream. Cover this with soaked sponge fingers and scatter over a little of the chopped almonds and glacé fruits. Repeat these layers until the tin is full. Cover with greased paper or foil and set in the refrigerator for 1–2 hours. Turn out and serve quite plain or with zabaione sauce.

Zabaione

yolks of 3 new-laid eggs
1 oz caster sugar
$2\frac{1}{2}$ tablespoons Marsala, or golden sherry

This popular Italian sweet (sometimes spelt zabaglione, or sabayon in French) can be served as a sauce for hot puddings as well as on its own in a warmed glass, such as a tall Claret goblet.

For large numbers make it in a copper mixing bowl and serve from this with a ladle straight into your party glasses.

Method

Put the yolks, sugar and Marsala, or sherry, in a pudding basin, sit this on a saucepan of hot water and then whisk steadily until the mixture thickens and rises. When very thick pour into warmed glasses and serve at once as it cannot be kept hot.

Savoy fingers, or thin slices of sponge cake baked in the oven until dry and crisp, go well with zabaione.

Gazpacho

1 cup (3 oz) white breadcrumbs
red wine vinegar (to taste)
2 cloves of garlic
salt
2 small ridge, or greenhouse, cucumbers
1 onion
1 green pepper
$\frac{1}{4}$ pint salad oil
2 lb tomatoes (rubbed through a sieve)
iced water
pepper

For serving
croûtons (made from toast)
bowl of ice cubes

Method

Soak the crumbs in 2 tablespoons vinegar. Pound the garlic to a cream with 1 teaspoon of salt. Roughly chop one cucumber, the onion and half the green pepper and put them, with the crumbs, into a mortar. Pound to a paste, then rub the paste through a fine sieve. Add the oil, a few drops at a time as for mayonnaise. Taste soup and season with a little more vinegar, if necessary, and pour into a tureen.

Add the tomatoes and some iced water. The amount of water depends on the juiciness of the tomatoes, but the soup should have a fairly thin consistency. Season and chill well.

The remaining cucumber and pepper, diced, may be added to the soup after chilling or served separately. Small croûtons and a bowl of ice cubes should be handed separately (in Spain, ice cubes are added to this traditional soup before it is drunk).

Spanish omelet 1

5 eggs (well beaten)
5 tablespoons olive oil
3 oz raw lean ham, or gammon rasher (chopped)
1 Spanish onion (thinly sliced)
1 clove of garlic (crushed with $\frac{1}{2}$ teaspoon salt) – optional
6 oz (about 2–3) potatoes (sliced, or coarsely grated)
salt and pepper

A true Spanish omelet is made on a base of potatoes and onion, then cooked in olive oil and well flavoured with garlic. Another version includes cooked mixed vegetables and is good for making use of left-overs. The consistency of both these omelets is firm, but not too solid.

This Spanish omelet, with ham and potatoes, is cut in wedges for serving with colourful peperoni

Method

Heat the oil in a frying pan, add the ham, or rasher, cook for a few minutes, then add the onion and a little of the crushed garlic to taste, if wished. Fry gently until the onion is half cooked, then add the potato. Season well; cook until soft.

Drain off any superfluous oil and add beaten eggs to pan. Stir to mix, then cook until the underneath of omelet is brown. When the mixture is barely set, slide the pan under the grill to brown the top surface. When well browned, turn out omelet on to a flat dish.

Cut into wedges and serve with peperoni.

Peperoni

2 green and 2 red peppers (halved, cored, seeds removed and thinly sliced)
1 oz butter
1 medium-size onion (sliced)
1 clove of garlic (crushed with pepper and $\frac{1}{2}$ teaspoon salt)

Method

Prepare the peppers and blanch if wished. Melt the butter in a small pan, add the onion and crushed garlic and cook slowly until soft but not coloured. Add the peppers and seasoning and cook until just tender.

Spanish omelet 2

5 eggs
4 tablespoons olive oil
2 cloves of garlic (whole)
$1\frac{1}{2}$ cups cooked mixed vegetables – small carrots, potatoes, sweet red peppers (all diced), peas
$\frac{1}{2}$ cup tomatoes (skinned, seeds removed and sliced)
salt and pepper

Method

Heat a large frying pan, put in the oil and garlic. Fry the garlic gently, then remove it. Put in the mixed vegetables and tomatoes and shake over heat until thoroughly hot.

Mix the eggs well with a fork in a basin, season and pour into the pan. Stir the mixture, then leave on gentle heat until the eggs are set.

Loosen omelet with a fish slice, then brown the surface under the grill. Slide omelet on to a flat serving dish.

Spanish lobster

1–1$\frac{1}{2}$ lb lobster meat, or
  1 large can (12 oz) claw meat
2–3 tablespoons olive oil
2 onions (finely sliced)
1 glass sherry (optional)
3–4 ripe tomatoes (skinned, quartered, seeds removed)
salt and pepper
about 1 wineglass stock
small bunch of chives
squeeze of lemon juice

Method

Heat the oil in a shallow pan, then add the onion. Lower the heat and stir occasionally until onion is tender and just turning colour. Then add the sherry (if using) and tomatoes. Season well and cook to a pulp. Put in the lobster, heat gently and add enough stock to moisten. There should be enough of this sauce to coat the lobster nicely. When hot, adjust the seasoning and snip in the chives. Add lemon juice and serve hot with buttered toast, or boiled rice.

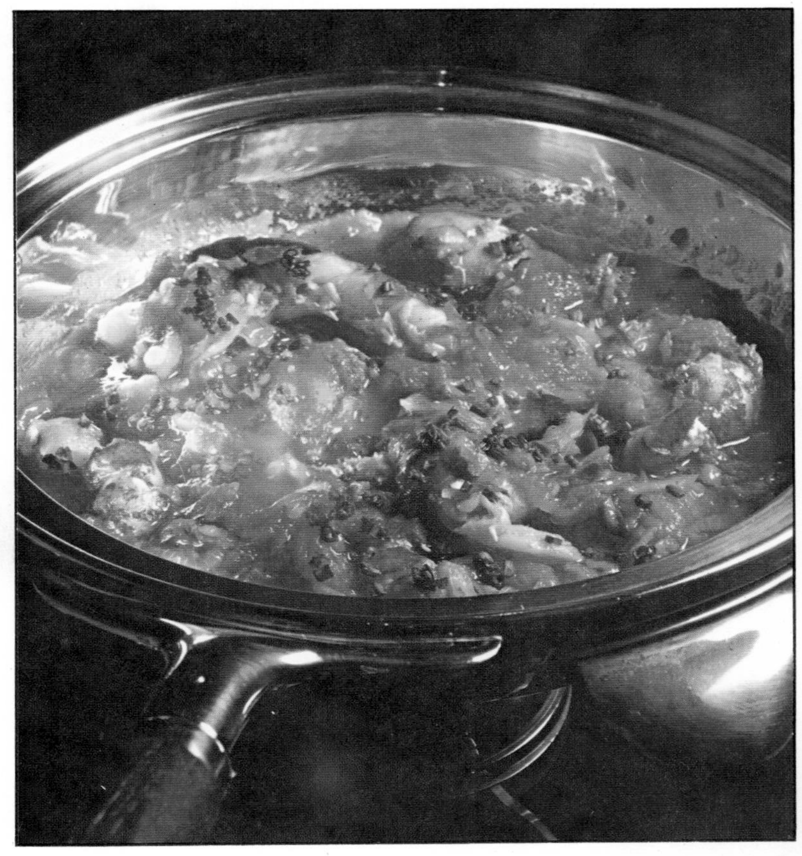

Paella

6 oz long grain rice
4 tablespoons olive oil
2–3 joints chicken, or rabbit (according to size)
1 onion (sliced)
1 clove of garlic (crushed with salt, or chopped)
4 oz gammon rasher (unsmoked and cut in strips)
½ lb firm white fish (halibut or cod) – skinned and cut in large squares
1 pint mussels
2–3 caps of canned pimiento (shredded)
½ pint prawns
1 cup peas (cooked), or small packet of frozen peas
1 large pinch of saffron (soaked in 2–3 tablespoons hot water)
1¼ pints stock, or water
salt and pepper

Anyone who has visited Spain will recognise this dish, and for those who have never sampled it, it is well worth trying. In Spain paella is both cooked and served in a special two-handled iron frying pan (paella) from which the dish gets the name. Here one can improvise with a large, deep frying pan, or sauté pan, or shallow flameproof casserole.

Paella is a colourful dish and the ingredients can be varied at will. For example, cooked chicken can be used or the mussels can be omitted, but the flavour and appearance will not be so good.

Method

Heat oil in a large frying pan, put in the pieces of chicken (or rabbit) and fry gently until they are coloured. Take out meat and add the onion and garlic to pan. Fry for a few minutes, then add the gammon and the rice. Fry rice, stirring continually, until it turns white. Then draw pan aside.

Have ready the fish, the mussels well scrubbed, the pimiento and the prawns – leave the heads on a few and set these aside. Arrange all these ingredients (except the reserved prawns) on the rice with the peas and the pieces of chicken (or rabbit) – these can be cut in half if too large.

Tuck the mussels well down in the pan and put the reserved prawns on the top. Add saffron and its liquid to the stock, pour this over the ingredients, season, cover with foil and a lid. Simmer rice gently on top of stove or put into the oven at 350°F or Mark 4 for 20–25 minutes, when all the ingredients should be cooked and the rice tender. Do not lift the lid during the cooking time. Serve very hot.

Watchpoint If your pan is thin, it is advisable to cook the paella in the oven, otherwise the rice may stick to the bottom.

Swiss cheese fondue

10–12 oz Swiss Emmenthal
10–12 oz Swiss Gruyère
1 clove of garlic (cut)
½ oz plain flour
2 wineglasses dry white wine
1 teaspoon lemon juice
1½ fl oz kirsch
grated nutmeg
black pepper (ground from mill)
French bread (for serving)

Method

Rub inside of pan with garlic. Grate cheeses and mix with flour, put into pan and add wine and lemon juice. Bring to boil over a moderate heat, stirring continuously in a figure of eight. Add kirsch, season with nutmeg and pepper, and bring back to boil. The fondue should be of a creamy consistency and is now ready to serve. Keep simmering throughout meal. Serve with French bread (retaining crust), cut into cubes.

Ingredients of Swiss delight: a fondue with small chunks of French bread, and a chilled light white wine

Trout à la genevoise

5–6 small, even-size trout
salt
1 wineglass water
4–6 peppercorns
$1\frac{1}{2}$ lb potatoes (cut into small balls and plainly boiled)

For sauce
1 small onion (finely chopped)
1 small carrot (finely chopped)
1 oz butter
2 wineglasses red wine
kneaded butter (made with $\frac{3}{4}$ oz butter and $\frac{1}{2}$ oz flour)
salt and pepper
dash of anchovy essence
a little thyme (chopped)
1 dessertspoon chopped parsley

The deep colouring of this rich sauce adds a lustre to the trout

Method

Set the oven at 350°F or Mark 4 and clean and trim the trout as usual. Butter an ovenproof dish well, lay in the trout and add a little salt, the water and peppercorns. Cover with a buttered paper and poach for about 15 minutes in the oven.

To make the sauce: sauté the onion and carrot in $\frac{1}{2}$ oz of butter, then add the wine and simmer until reduced to half quantity. Strain off the liquor from the trout and add to the pan. Simmer for 4–5 minutes, thicken slightly with kneaded butter, reboil, adjust seasoning and add the anchovy essence, thyme, remaining butter and parsley. Spoon sauce over trout; serve with potato balls.

Chicken à la suisse

$3\frac{1}{2}$ lb roasting chicken
4 thin rashers of streaky bacon
1 large onion (thinly sliced)
2 large carrots (thinly sliced)
1 stick of celery (sliced)
$2\frac{1}{2}$ fl oz stock (made from chicken giblets)
bouquet garni
$\frac{1}{2}$ lb noodles
1 oz butter
pepper (ground from mill)
$\frac{1}{2}$ oz Parmesan cheese (grated)

For cheese sauce
1 oz butter
1 oz plain flour
$\frac{3}{4}$ pint flavoured milk
2 oz Emmenthal, or Gruyère, cheese (grated)
salt and pepper
2–3 tablespoons double cream

Method

Lay the bacon on the bottom of a deep pan, cover with the onion, carrot and celery and set the trussed chicken on top. Cover the pan and cook over very gentle heat for 10–15 minutes. Pour the stock over the chicken, tuck in the herbs with the vegetables, cover again and cook gently, either on top of the stove or in the oven at 325–350°F or Mark 3–4, for about 50–60 minutes.

Meanwhile curl the noodles into a large pan of boiling

Chicken joints on noodles have been coated with sauce and grated cheese before browning under the grill

Chicken à la suisse continued

salted water, reduce the heat a little and boil until just tender; drain, refresh and put back into the rinsed pan with ½ pint hand-hot water.

Prepare the sauce as for a béchamel, then beat in the grated Emmenthal (or Gruyère) a little at a time and taste for seasoning. Add the cream and keep the sauce warm.

Take up the chicken, reduce the gravy a little and strain. Skim off as much fat as possible, then add the liquid to the cheese sauce. Drain the noodles and heat them in the butter, adding plenty of pepper from the mill before tipping into a hot flameproof serving dish. Carve the chicken, arrange joints on top of the noodles and coat with the sauce. Dust with the grated Parmesan and brown lightly under the grill.

The noodles for the chicken à la suisse are tossed in freshly ground black pepper and butter

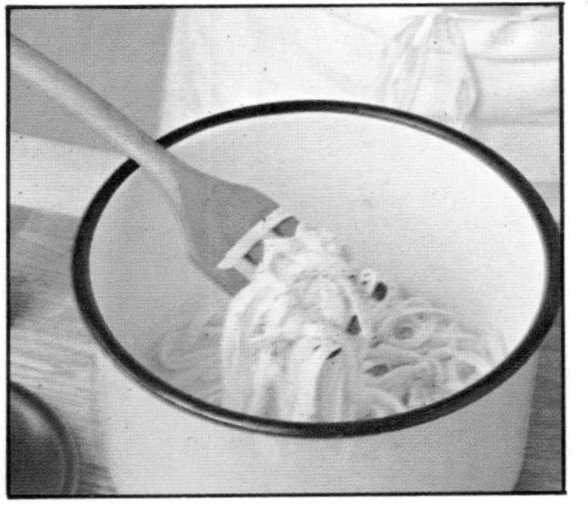

Salé
(Swiss cheese dish)

For rich shortcrust pastry
6 oz plain flour
pinch of salt
3 oz butter
1 oz shortening
1 egg yolk
2 tablespoons cold water

For filling
½ pint béchamel sauce
little double cream
3 eggs
4½ oz Gruyère cheese (grated)
salt and pepper
grated nutmeg

7-inch diameter flan ring

Method
Make the rich shortcrust pastry (see page 21), and set aside to chill. When chilled, line the pastry on to the flan ring. Make the béchamel sauce (but add a little cream to it) and when cool beat in the eggs and grated cheese; add plenty of seasoning and a grating of nutmeg. Pour the mixture into the pastry case and bake for about 25 minutes in an oven at 375–400°F or Mark 5–6.

Eastern Europe

When East meets West, as in Greece, Russia and Hungary, it is reflected in the food. The frugal, carefully cooked food of Greece and Hungary is flavoured with herbs and spices from Turkey, and the wide variety of foods provided by the diversity of the Russian landscape and climate is also traditionally more spiced and richly dressed than the same foods would be in Western Europe.

In all three countries vegetables are given a more important place than in British cuisine – hence the delicious sweet and spicy beetroot soups from Russia and Greece's famous dolmas (true dolmas are made with vine leaves, but cabbage leaves make a good substitute). Hungarian marrow is another dish where a good vegetable makes a small supply of meat go a long way in a good and tasty meal. And only in the glorious warmth of mediterranean Greece could the bitter lemon be turned into a delicious cool soup for a hot and dusty day.

Greek lemon soup (Avgolemono)

thinly pared rind and juice of 1 small lemon
good oz butter
3 shallots (finely chopped)
1 rounded tablespoon plain flour
2 pints jellied chicken stock
2–3 egg yolks
3–4 tablespoons double cream (lightly whipped)

For garnish
1 egg white
1–2 tablespoons cream, or top of the milk
salt and pepper

Method

Melt butter in a pan, add chopped shallots, cover and cook very slowly for 2–3 minutes, but do not allow them to colour. Draw pan aside, stir in the flour, blend in the stock and bring to the boil. Simmer for 10 minutes, then add the thinly pared rind of the lemon and the strained juice.

Watchpoint Care must be taken that this soup is not too sharp in flavour. To prevent this, add the lemon juice to taste.

Continue to simmer the soup for a further 7–10 minutes. Then strain liquid, return to the rinsed-out pan and draw aside.

Meanwhile set the oven at 325°F or Mark 3. Lightly beat the egg white for the garnish with a fork just to break it, add the cream (or milk) with the seasoning. Turn into an individual soufflé dish or cocotte. Bake this in pre-set oven for 7–10 minutes, or until firm to the touch, leave until cold and turn out, slice and cut out into tiny rounds, or diamonds.

Mix the egg yolks together, add a little of the warm soup, then add this mixture to the soup as for a liaison. Reheat, stirring constantly, but do not allow to boil. Then add the lightly whipped cream and the egg white garnish just before serving. If serving soup chilled, after adding liaison cool it and put in refrigerator. The garnish should not be added until just before serving.

Moussaka

12 oz cold cooked lamb
1 medium-size onion (finely chopped)
$\frac{3}{4}$ oz butter
3–4 tablespoons tomato sauce (see page 49)
salt and pepper
1 clove of garlic (crushed with $\frac{1}{2}$ teaspoon salt)
pinch of grated nutmeg, or ground mace
1 aubergine (sliced, dégorgé)
3–4 tablespoons oil
2–3 potatoes (boiled in their skins, peeled and sliced)
$\frac{1}{2}$ lb tomatoes (peeled and sliced)

For béchamel sauce
$\frac{3}{4}$ oz butter
1 tablespoon plain flour
$7\frac{1}{2}$ fl oz milk (infused with 1 slice of onion, 2–3 peppercorns, 1 blade of mace and 2–3 parsley stalks)
little mustard
1 egg (separated)
$\frac{1}{2}$ oz cheese (grated)

Method

Slice the meat and cut into neat dice. Soften the onion in the butter, add the meat and moisten with tomato sauce. Season and add garlic, nutmeg or mace.

Have ready the aubergine. Drain, dry and fry in oil, then remove the slices. Arrange meat mixture, potatoes, tomatoes and aubergine in layers in a hot ovenproof dish (see photograph).

Prepare béchamel sauce, then add mustard. Beat in egg yolk, whip white to a firm snow and fold into mixture with the cheese. Spoon it over moussaka and brown in oven at 400°F or Mark 6 for 10–15 minutes.

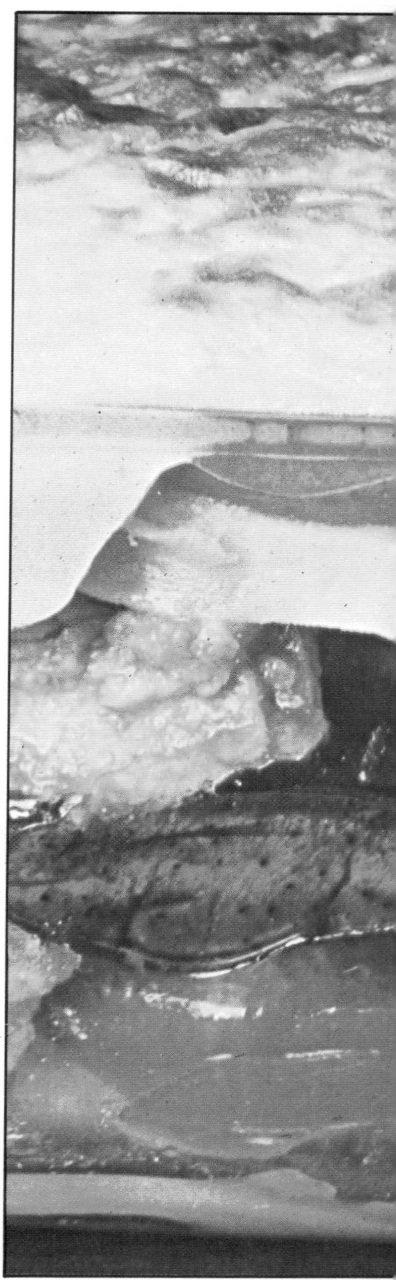

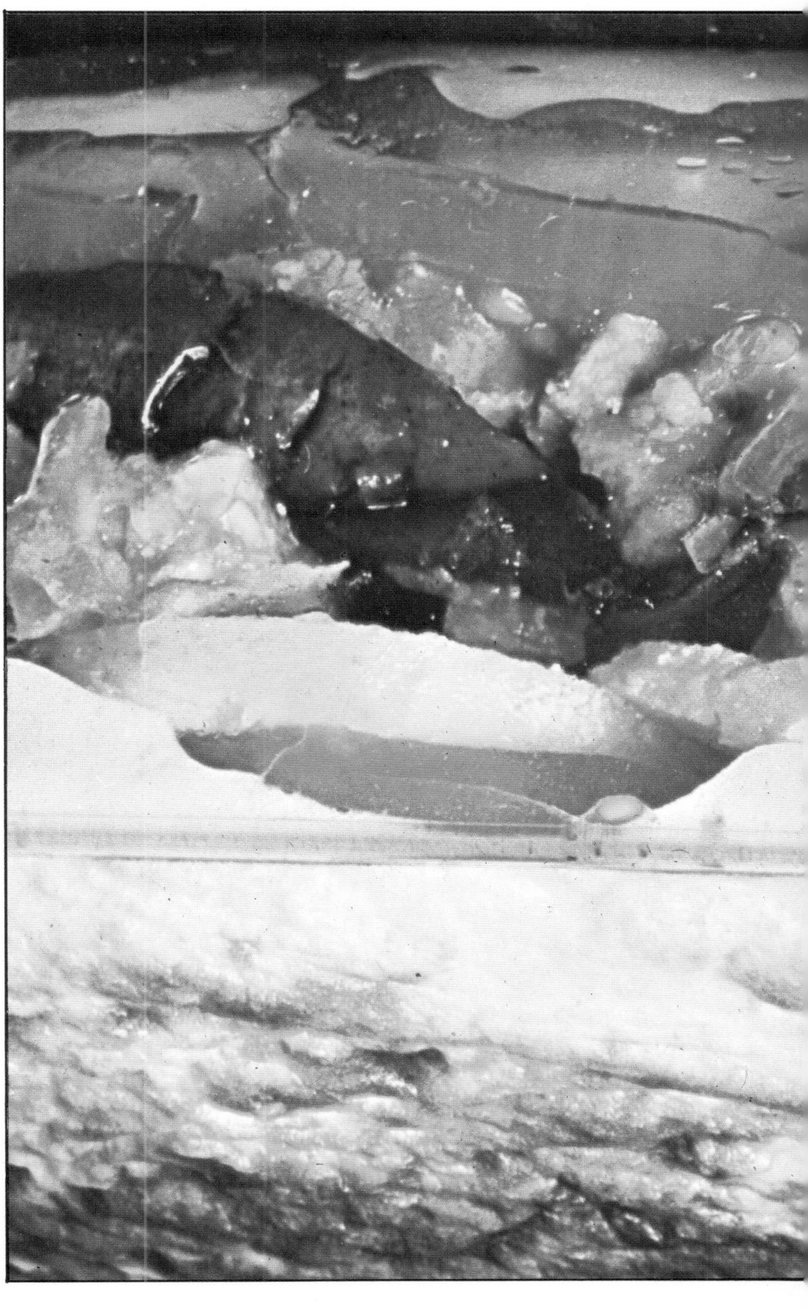

Dolmas au chou
(or Dolmades)

6 oz raw beef (minced)
1 small onion (finely chopped)
salt and pepper
5 tablespoons water
2 tablespoons rice (cooked)
1 cabbage
flour
brown stock
1 bayleaf
$\frac{1}{2}$–$\frac{3}{4}$ pint tomato sauce (see page 49)
parsley (chopped)

Method
Put onion into a bowl with the meat and seasoning. Work well together, adding the water gradually until the mixture is well beaten and pliable. Stir in rice and adjust seasoning.

Trim the cabbage, blanch it whole in boiling water for 2–3 minutes, drain well, then carefully detach the leaves, removing any hard stalk.

Put a small tablespoon of the mixture on each leaf, roll up like a parcel to form a sausage shape. Then roll very lightly in flour and arrange in criss-cross layers in a thick pan or flameproof casserole. Barely cover with stock, bring carefully to the boil, season, add a bayleaf and simmer for 20-30 minutes on the stove, or in the oven at 350°F or Mark 4.

Thin tomato sauce with water. Carefully lift the dolmas into ovenproof dish, draining well from the liquor, pour over the tomato sauce and cook in the oven at 350°F or Mark 4 for a further 20–30 minutes.

Sprinkle well with chopped parsley before serving dolmas.

Hungarian eggs

5 eggs (hard-boiled and sliced)
4 small onions (thinly sliced)
$\frac{1}{2}$ lb tomatoes (skinned and sliced with seeds removed)
paprika pepper
about 1 oz tomato butter (to garnish)

This is an easy and quick dish to make; and the tomato butter gives it an unusual touch.

Method
Fry the sliced onions until golden-brown. Add the prepared tomatoes and simmer for 4–5 minutes.

Put the sliced eggs in the serving dish, cover with the tomato mixture and dust with paprika. Garnish the top with round flat pats of tomato butter.

Tomato butter

Work together 1 oz or more of butter, 1 teaspoon tomato purée, salt and pepper and 2–3 drops of Worcestershire sauce. Chill and shape into pats each about the size of a 10p piece.

Escalopes of veal hongroise

3–4 veal escalopes
1 tablespoon seasoned flour
1–2 tablespoons olive oil
1 teaspoon paprika pepper
1 glass Marsala, or brown sherry
about $\frac{1}{4}$ pint jellied stock

For salpicon
1 aubergine
2 tablespoons olive oil
1 large onion (finely sliced)
1 teaspoon paprika pepper
2 caps of canned pimiento (shredded)

Method

Slice the aubergine, sprinkle with salt and leave 10–15 minutes to 'dégorger'.

Cut the escalopes in half to form scaloppine and roll in the flour. Heat the oil in a sauté pan and brown the veal on both sides. Reduce the heat, blend in the paprika and cook for 1 minute. Pour on the Marsala or sherry and let it boil until reduced to almost nothing.

Add 2 tablespoons jellied stock, cover the pan and simmer gently for 7–10 minutes. Extra stock may be added during this time if needed, but the veal should be coated with a sticky glaze and not lying in a sauce.

Heat the oil in a frying pan, wipe the aubergine slices on kitchen paper and cook until coloured on both sides. Remove from pan and keep warm. Cook onion slowly in pan until golden, with extra oil if needed. Stir in paprika and pimiento and reserve juice from pan.

Return the aubergine slices to the pan, spoon over a little pimiento juice, season, cover and cook gently until tender.

Serve the scaloppine on the salpicon or in a separate dish.

Hungarian marrow

1 small young marrow
1–2 oz butter
1 dessertspoon paprika pepper
1 small onion (finely chopped)
2–3 tablespoons wine vinegar
about 6 dill, or caraway, seeds
1 teaspoon caster sugar
kneaded butter

Method

Peel marrow, cut into quarters, scoop out seeds and slice thinly. Melt 1–2 oz butter in a large pan. Put in the marrow and fry quickly for 4–5 minutes, shaking the pan well. Add the paprika. Take out the marrow and put in the onion, with more butter, if necessary.

Cover the pan for 1–2 minutes to cook the onion, then add the vinegar, dill (or caraway) seeds and the sugar. Thicken slightly with kneaded butter, replace the marrow, cover and simmer for 5 minutes, by which time it should be just tender.

Shoulder of veal hongroise

$2\frac{1}{2}$ lb shoulder of veal
2 cloves of garlic (crushed)
1 dessertspoon paprika pepper
2 oz butter
1 bayleaf
1 shallot (finely chopped)
$\frac{1}{2}$–$\frac{3}{4}$ pint veal, or chicken, stock
salt and pepper
3 tomatoes
2 caps of pimiento (canned)
1 tablespoon plain flour
2–3 tablespoons plain yoghourt

Method

Crush the garlic to a paste with the paprika and $\frac{1}{2}$ oz of the butter. Then, with a sharp-pointed knife, make about 12 incisions over the surface of the joint. Work the paste well into these.

Heat remaining butter in a roasting tin in the oven set at 375°F or Mark 5, put in the meat and baste well. Add bay-leaf, shallot, $\frac{1}{2}$ pint stock and a little seasoning to the roasting tin and put in the oven for $1\frac{1}{2}$ hours. Baste veal every 15 minutes, and turn it half way through the cooking time.

Scald and skin the tomatoes, cut in four, scoop out the seeds and then cut again. Slice the pimientos. Take up the meat, turn electric oven off or gas oven to its lowest setting.

Carve the meat and arrange in an entrée dish; keep warm. Strain the liquid from the roasting tin; measure and make up to $\frac{1}{2}$ pint with extra stock or water, if necessary. Skim the fat from the top of the liquid, blend with the flour to make a smooth paste and mix into the stock in a saucepan. Stir until boiling, add the prepared tomato and pimiento and simmer for 2–3 minutes; taste for seasoning. Spoon this sauce over the meat.

Beat the yoghourt lightly with a fork and pour over the top of the meat. Cover the dish with a lid or foil and put back in the warm oven for 15–20 minutes.

Serve with noodles, or new potatoes tossed in butter and chopped parsley. Carrots mixed with cucumber – cucumber Vichy – make a delicious accompaniment.

Working the butter, paprika and garlic paste into the joint of veal so that it penetrates through incisions in meat

Paprika goulash

$1\frac{1}{2}$ lb chuck, or blade bone, steak
2 tablespoons dripping, or oil
8 oz onions (sliced)
1 tablespoon paprika pepper
1 tablespoon plain flour
1 dessertspoon tomato purée (canned, or in tube)
$\frac{3}{4}$–1 pint brown stock
bouquet garni
1 clove of garlic (crushed)
salt and pepper
1 sweet pepper (red or green), or 1 cap of canned pimiento
2 large tomatoes
4 tablespoons soured cream

Goulash, or gulyás, is a Hungarian stew, generally of beef flavoured with paprika. If lamb and pork are used, the dish may be called pörkölt. Gulyás means 'herdsmen's stew' and probably originated with the nomadic herdsmen's habit of cooking in a large single pot over the camp fire.

Method

Cut meat into large squares, brown quickly in pan of hot dripping or oil and take out. Lower heat and put in sliced onions; after 3–4 minutes, add paprika. Cook slowly for 1 minute, then add flour, tomato pureé and stock. Stir until boiling, replace meat, add bouquet garni, garlic and seasoning. Cover and simmer gently for 2 hours, or until meat is very tender, on top of stove or in the oven at 325°F or Mark 3.

Blanch, peel and shred the pepper; scald and peel the tomatoes, remove hard core and seeds, then slice flesh. Now add to goulash together with the pepper. Bring slowly to the boil and dish up.

Spoon over a little sour cream and stir in gently. Serve with boiled potatoes or noodles.

Hungarian pancakes
(Crêpes hongroise)

½ pint pancake batter

For filling
1 lb spinach
1½ oz butter
1 shallot (finely chopped)
4 tomatoes
2 teaspoons tomato purée
1 teaspoon paprika pepper
4 eggs (hard-boiled)
salt
pepper (ground from mill)

For topping
melted butter
½ oz Parmesan cheese (grated)

Method
Prepare the batter and leave to stand in a cool place for 30 minutes.

Meanwhile prepare filling: cook the spinach in plenty of boiling salted water, drain well and keep on one side.

Melt 1 oz butter in a pan, add the shallot and cook slowly until soft but not coloured. Scald and skin tomatoes, squeeze out seeds and chop the flesh. Stir in the tomato purée and paprika and simmer for 2–3 minutes. Add the hard-boiled eggs and season.

Fry paper-thin pancakes and cover the surface of each with the leaf spinach heated through in about ½ oz butter. Place about a tablespoon of the egg mixture on each pancake and roll up. Place them in a hot flameproof serving dish, sprinkle with melted butter and grated cheese and brown lightly under the grill. Serve at once.

Basic pancake batter

4 oz plain flour
pinch of salt
1 egg
1 egg yolk
½ pint of milk
1 tablespoon butter (melted), or olive oil

6-inch diameter frying pan

Method
Sift the flour with the salt into a bowl, make a well in the centre, add the egg and yolk and begin to add the milk slowly, stirring all the time. When half the milk has been added, stir in the melted butter or oil and beat well until smooth. Add the remaining milk and leave to stand for 30 minutes before using. The batter should have the consistency of thin cream; if too thick, add a little extra milk.

Heat frying pan. Grease very lightly with butter or oil and put a good tablespoon of batter in the middle. Roll the pan to coat the surface evenly, then keep over brisk heat until the pancake is brown on the underside. Loosen round the edge with a palette knife and toss or turn over and brown the other side.

Slide the pancake on to a wire cake rack. As the pancakes are made, stack them one on top of the other and, if being fried several hours before they are needed, wrap them in a clean tea towel until wanted. Allow two pancakes per person.

Bortschok

2 lb shin of beef
4 pints water
2 onions (1 stuck with a clove)
large bouquet garni
parsley stalks
1 bayleaf
stick of celery
strip of lemon peel
6 peppercorns
1 teaspoon salt
3 large cooked beetroots
1 can consommé (optional)
$9\frac{1}{2}$–10 fl oz soured cream (optional)

Method

Cut up the beef into small pieces and put in a large pan with three-quarters of the water; bring slowly to the boil, removing the scum as it rises, and add the remaining water in two parts. This addition of cold water brings the scum more rapidly to the surface and makes the broth clear. When on boiling point and well skimmed, put in the rest of the ingredients (except the beetroot, consommé and soured cream), partly cover the pan and allow to simmer for about 3 hours.

Note: If using a solid fuel cooker, cover the pan completely and put in the cool oven overnight.

Strain the broth and return to a clean pan. Grate the beetroot and add to the broth. Cover the pan and leave to infuse on low heat for about 40 minutes. Test for seasoning; the soup should not taste sweet but have a strong flavour of beetroot. Sharpen with a few drops of vinegar, or lemon juice, salt and sugar. The addition of these last two gives a piquant flavour. Then strain the soup through a piece of muslin. If wished, add the consommé at this stage.

Serve the soup in cups with a bowl of soured cream handed separately, if wished. Serve the hot pirozhki separately.

Pirozhki

8 oz plain flour
1 teaspoon salt
scant $\frac{1}{2}$ oz yeast
1 teaspoon sugar
3–4 tablespoons milk
2 eggs
2 oz butter

For filling
1 small onion (chopped)
1 oz butter
2 oz mushrooms (sliced), or $\frac{1}{2}$ oz dried mushrooms
2 eggs (hard-boiled and chopped)
3 oz long grain rice (boiled until tender, drained and dried)
salt and pepper
beaten egg

Method

Sift the flour with the salt into a warm bowl. Work the yeast with the sugar, then add the milk, warmed to blood heat. Whisk the eggs and add to the flour with the yeast mixture, beating well with your hand. The dough should be rather soft, a little more so than for a scone dough. Then cream the butter, add to the dough and cover the basin with a plate. Leave in the refrigerator overnight; at the end of this time the dough should have risen to the top of the basin and will be firm enough to handle easily.

To make the filling: soften the onion in a pan with the butter, add the mushrooms and cook briskly for 2–3 minutes; turn into a bowl and mix with eggs and rice. Season well. If wished, this mixture may be bound with a little beaten egg for easy handling.

Roll out the dough and stamp it out into rounds about $2\frac{1}{2}$ inches in diameter: put a spoonful of the filling in the centre of each round, and brush with beaten egg; bring the edges up over the top and pinch well together. Prove in a warm place for 7–10 minutes and, when lightly risen, fry in deep fat on a rising temperature to allow pies to cook through without overbrowning the surface. If preferred they may be fried some time before they are wanted, then put into a hot oven for 4–5 minutes to heat them through. Alternatively, brush with beaten egg and bake in a hot oven (400°F or Mark 6).

Bortschok served with hot pirozhki and soured cream

Vegetable bortsch

beetroot
onions
carrots
celery
1 parsnip
salt and pepper
stock (preferably ham), or water
cabbage (coarsely shredded)
garlic (chopped, or crushed) – to taste
tomatoes
sugar
little tomato purée
fresh parsley (chopped)

For liaison
little flour (optional)
soured cream

5-inch diameter pudding basin (sufficient for 3 pints liquid), or small mixing bowl

Quantities of vegetables should be used in the following proportions: half beetroot and of remaining half, one-third onion, one-third carrot and the last third equally divided between celery and parsnip.

Bortsch (spelt borshch in Russian) is the national soup of the Ukraine, the name being an old Slav word for beet. There are numerous ways of making bortsch but it always contains root vegetables with a large proportion of beetroot, and sometimes up to three kinds of meat.

Method

Cut beetroot, onions, carrots, celery and parsnip into matchsticks and pack into the basin or bowl to fill it.

Lightly season stock or water and bring to the boil. Turn the bowl of vegetables into the pan, cover and simmer for about 20–30 minutes. Coarsely shred enough cabbage to fill the bowl, add this with the garlic to taste. Continue to simmer gently, uncovered, for a further 20 minutes.

Skin sufficient tomatoes to half-fill the bowl, squeeze to remove seeds, then chop flesh very coarsely. Add to soup, season well with salt and sugar and add a little tomato purée to sharpen the flavour. Simmer for a further 10 minutes, then add a handful of chopped parsley.

The soup can be thickened lightly with a little flour mixed with a small quantity of soured cream. Otherwise serve a bowl of soured cream separately.

Watchpoint Bortsch should be slightly piquant in flavour and not sweet. Add salt and sugar until this is reached. The soup should be a thick broth of vegetables but not too solid. Dilute if necessary with additional stock.

This bortsch is improved if made the previous day.

Pheasant smetana

2 pheasants (a brace, or
  2 hen birds)
good oz butter
2 shallots (chopped)
1 wineglass white wine
salt and pepper

For sauce
3 shallots (finely chopped)
1 large wineglass dry white wine
1 dessertspoon plain flour
$7\frac{1}{2}$ fl oz lightly soured cream
  (fresh cream with a little lemon
  juice added may be substituted)

Method

Heat the butter in a large pan, and slowly brown the birds all over. Then add shallots and wine, season, cover and simmer gently on top of the stove for 35–40 minutes, turning the birds over from time to time.

When birds are cooked, pour off the gravy from the pan and reserve it, leaving birds in pan, covered. To prepare the sauce, cook shallots in the wine in a saucepan until the wine has reduced by half, then pour off and set aside. Skim the butter from the reserved gravy, put it into the saucepan and stir in the flour. Strain in the gravy, add the reduced wine and the cream. Season well and boil until sauce is thick and creamy. Draw pan aside.

Take up pheasants, carve into joints and dish up. Reheat sauce and strain over the dish. Serve very hot with boiled rice and French beans.

Beef Stroganov

$1\frac{1}{2}$ lb fillet of beef
2–3 onions (sliced)
butter (for frying)
6 oz mushrooms (sliced)
salt and pepper
1 cup soured cream, or fresh double cream soured with juice of $\frac{1}{2}$ lemon

Method

Cut the fillet into strips about the size of your small finger and set aside. Fry the onions slowly in butter until golden-brown lift out with a slice and keep warm. Fry mushrooms and keep warm with the onions. Increase the heat and fry the steak very quickly for 3–4 minutes on each side, taking care that the juice does not run. To avoid this, fry the meat in two lots so that the temperature is not lowered too much. Return all meat to the pan, season well, add the onions and mushrooms and shake up over the heat. Pour in the soured cream, bring quickly to the boil and serve with plainly boiled rice.

Beef Stroganov is an ideal recipe to prepare in a chafing dish

Apricot moscovite

½ lb apricots (poached until tender in a syrup made from ½ pint water and 3 oz granulated sugar) – soak dried apricots overnight before poaching
½ pint milk
3 egg yolks
3 oz caster sugar
scant ½ oz gelatine
¼ pint double cream (lightly whipped)
3–4 tablespoons brandy (optional)

For decoration (optional)
extra double cream (whipped)
praline powder

Jelly mould (1–1½ pint capacity)

Praline powder
Melt 3 oz caster sugar with 3 oz unblanched almonds in a pan over low heat. When turning pale golden-brown, stir with a metal spoon until nut-brown. Turn on to an oiled tin or plate, and leave until hard. Crush into coarse powder with a rolling pin, or use a nut mill, mincer or grinder (makes about 5 tablespoons). Store in an airtight container.

Method

Scald the milk, cream the egg yolks with the sugar, pour on the scalded milk, blend and then return custard to pan. Thicken over heat without boiling, strain and cool.

Drain the apricots, reserving the syrup, and rub them through a nylon strainer. Divide this pureé into two and put one half in the refrigerator to chill.

Dissolve the gelatine over gentle heat in 2½ fl oz of the apricot syrup and add it to the egg custard. Add the chilled apricot purée to the cream. When the custard is on the point of setting, fold in the apricot cream, flavour with 1–2 tablespoons brandy, and turn into the oiled mould to set.

Flavour the remaining purée with the rest of the brandy to make an apricot sauce and add the reserved syrup. Turn out the mould on to a serving dish, decorate with a little extra cream and praline, and pour around the sauce.

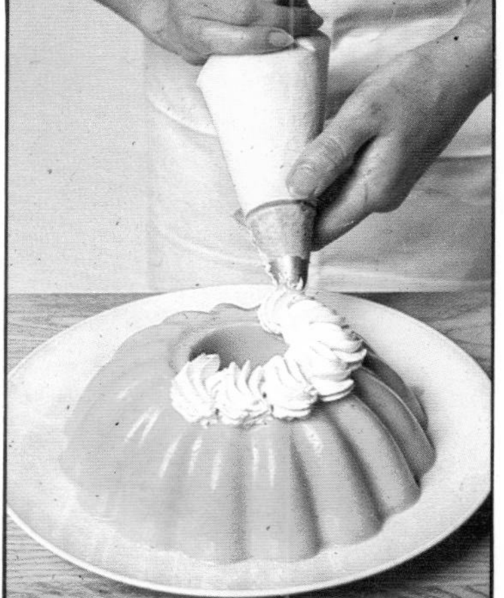

Piping the whipped cream on to the apricot mould after turning it out

Russian tipsy cake

1 oz unsweetened chocolate
3 tablespoons water
3 eggs
$4\frac{1}{2}$ oz caster sugar
$2\frac{1}{4}$ oz plain flour (very well sifted with a pinch of salt)
1 tablespoon plain flour
2–3 tablespoons sugar syrup (flavoured with 2–3 tablespoons brandy, or rum)
$\frac{1}{2}$ pint double cream
a few drops of vanilla essence
2 oz block chocolate (for making caraque)

8–9 inch diameter sandwich tin

Method

Prepare the tin (grease with some melted shortening, then dust with caster sugar and with sifted flour) and set the oven at 375°F or Mark 5. Melt the chocolate in the water until it forms a thick cream, then leave it to cool.

To make the sponge cake: whisk the eggs and sugar together in a bowl over a pan of hot water (or use an electric mixer at high speed, without heat) until thick and mousse-like. Remove from the heat and whisk until mixture is cold. Fold in the flour. Divide the mixture in two and add the prepared chocolate to one portion and the extra tablespoon of flour to the other.

Put the two mixtures into the prepared tin, alternating spoonfuls of light and dark. Draw a knife through to give a marbled effect and bake in the pre-set oven for 40–50 minutes or until the cake tests done (it must spring back immediately when pressed with the finger).

When the cake is cool, split it and spoon a little of the flavoured syrup over both halves. Whip and sweeten the cream and flavour it with vanilla essence. Fill the cake with cream, reserving some for decoration. Reshape the cake and moisten it with any remaining syrup. Decorate the cake with chocolate caraque and rosettes of cream.

The tipsy cake is decorated with scrolls of chocolate caraque as well as whipped double cream

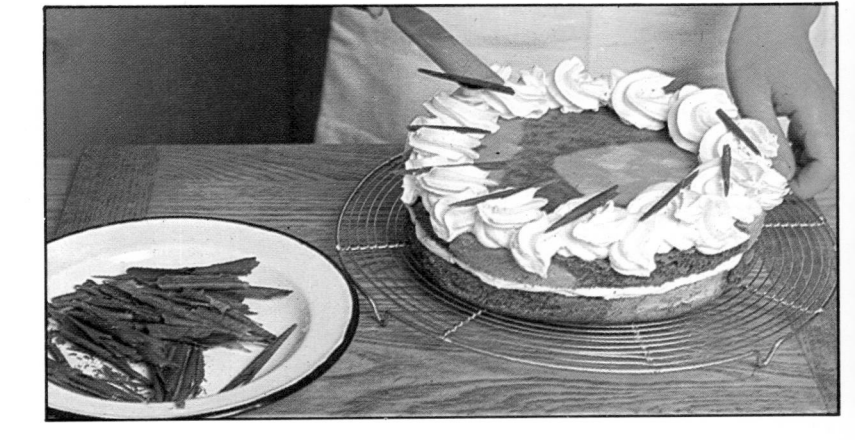

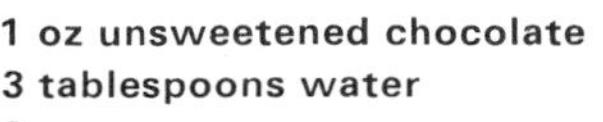

Scandinavia

Herrings with dill, meat cooked in butter, sauces made with cream – nothing could be more typical of Scandinavian cooking, except perhaps the delicious cakes and fruit preserves.

Although the four countries that make up the area known as Scandinavia each have their own national dishes, in many respects their cooking is similar. Everywhere there is an abundance of fresh fish and dairy products; pork is the favourite meat – the one always served at Christmas for instance – and in Finland and Norway, the mountains provide a ready source of game. Swedish, Danish and Norwegian housewives also make a lot of fruit preserves – their favourite fruit seems to be wild cranberries, which unfortunately are almost unobtainable in Britain.

Traditionally the cooking is done with butter rather than oil, and milk and cream are frequently added to sauces and soups. The Danes particularly are very proud of their cakes and cookies, which always have the characteristic flavour of butter.

The traditional smørgasbørd is rather substantial for modern British appetites, but we can make good use of the Danish open sandwich. This is more of a meal on a slice of bread than the English bread-with-something type of sandwich; it is ideal for informal entertaining and for family meals.

Iced apple and apricot cream soup

1 lb fresh apricots, or $\frac{1}{2}$ lb dried apricots (soaked overnight in 1 pint boiling water)
2 lb cooking apples (peeled, quartered and cored)
$\frac{1}{2}$ pint strong beef stock
1 bayleaf
few sprigs of parsley
2 sticks of celery
salt and pepper
1$\frac{1}{2}$ pints milk
double cream (for serving)

Method

Wash the apricots and place in a pan with the apples, stock, herbs, celery and seasoning and bring to the boil. Cover the pan and simmer gently for 20–30 minutes or until the fruit is quite soft. Remove the celery, parsley and bayleaf and rub the soup through a fine sieve or work in a blender.

Season soup carefully and stir in the milk. Dilute the soup, if necessary, with more milk. Chill and serve with double cream, whipped with a little salt.

Swedish roll mop salad

3–4 roll mop herrings
1 lb new potatoes
oil and vinegar dressing (made with 6 tablespoons olive oil and 2 tablespoons white wine vinegar)
1–2 dill cucumbers (sliced)
2 tablespoons freshly chopped dill

Method

Boil the new potatoes with the skins on. Peel them while hot, then quarter or slice them, according to size, and moisten with the dressing. Leave to cool.

Cut the roll mops into shreds; mix these and the cucumber slices with the potatoes, adding more dressing, if necessary, and the fresh dill. Pile salad in a dish for serving.

Pigeons with cranberry cream sauce

4 pigeons
1 oz butter
1 shallot (finely chopped)
1 tablespoon plain flour
$\frac{1}{2}$ pint jellied stock
salt and pepper
6 oz fresh cranberries and 1 tablespoon sugar, or 1 can cranberry sauce
3–4 tablespoons double cream

Method

Set oven at 350°F or Mark 4.

Brown the pigeons slowly in the butter in a flameproof casserole. Remove and split each bird in half and cut away the backbone and leg joints (use to make game soup).

Add the shallot to the pan and cook slowly until golden. Stir in flour, allow to colour; tip on stock, season, stir until boiling.

Replace the pigeons in the pan and add the fresh cranberries and sugar (or the canned cranberry sauce). Cover and cook in the moderate pre-set oven for about 1 hour. Take up the pigeons and reserve. Rub the sauce through a strainer, or work in a blender, until smooth.

Replace the pigeons in the casserole, pour over the sauce and add cream. Reheat in oven for a few minutes before serving.

Savoury Danish ring

12 oz plain flour
large pinch of salt
1 oz yeast
1 oz caster sugar.
$7\frac{1}{2}$ fl oz warm milk
9 oz butter
1 egg (beaten)

For filling
1 large onion (finely chopped)
2 oz butter
3 tablespoons breadcrumbs
salt and pepper
2 tablespoons ground almonds
2 tablespoons grated Parmesan cheese
$\frac{1}{2}$ beaten egg

To finish
$\frac{1}{2}$ beaten egg
1 tablespoon grated Parmesan cheese
1 tablespoon poppy, or sesame, seeds

Angel cake tin

Method

Sift the flour with the salt into a mixing bowl. Cream the yeast with the sugar until liquid. Add the warm milk and 2 oz of the butter and stir until dissolved; then add the beaten egg. Pour the liquid ingredients into the flour and mix to a smooth dough. Cover and leave at room temperature for about 1 hour, or until double in bulk.

Punch down the dough, turn it on to a floured board and knead lightly. Roll out to an oblong and cover two-thirds of the dough with half the remaining butter, divided in small pieces the size of a walnut, fold and roll as for flaky pastry. Fold in three and roll again. Put on remaining butter, fold and leave for 15 minutes. Roll and fold twice more, wrap in a clean tea towel and leave in the refrigerator for at least 15 minutes, but preferably 30 minutes, while preparing the filling.

For the filling: cook the onion in the butter until soft and golden, then add the bread-crumbs and season well. Tip into a bowl, work in the ground almonds and cheese and bind with a little beaten egg. Allow to cool.

Roll out the chilled dough to a large oblong, spread over the filling, roll up dough and join the ends to make a circle. Place in a very lightly buttered angel cake tin and prove in a warm place for 10–15 minutes, until well risen. Brush with beaten egg, dust with the Parmesan cheese and poppy or sesame seeds and bake in a hot oven, pre-set at 400°F or Mark 6.

When cold, cut the ring into slices for serving.

Above: rolling up chilled dough before proving
Below: savoury Danish ring, dusted with Parmesan cheese and poppy seeds

Danish open sandwiches

These are useful for informal party entertaining or casual family meals. Their charm, when eaten, is that they have plenty of topping on very little bread

Luncheon meat

pork luncheon meat (sliced)
rye crispbread (buttered)
horseradish cream (made with 2 tablespoons horseradish sauce, 1 teaspoon sugar, a squeeze of lemon juice and a 6 fl oz can of Danish cream)
lettuce heart
1 orange (sliced)
2 cooked prunes (stoned) for each slice of bread

Method

Fold each slice of luncheon meat in half and arrange on the buttered crispbread, using 3 slices for each sandwich. Put a spoonful of horseradish cream on the top, with a small piece of lettuce heart beside it. Twist the slice of orange and place it as in the chicken and bacon recipe, between two prunes.

Salami

salami (thinly sliced)
wheatmeal bread (sliced and buttered)
lettuce leaves
4–5 onion rings for each slice of bread
small cress

Method

Cover the bread with a lettuce leaf, fold each slice of salami loosely in half and place 4 on each slice of bread, with onion rings and small cress.

Chicken and bacon

chicken joints
white bread (sliced and buttered)
lettuce leaves
1 streaky bacon roll (grilled) for each slice of bread
1 orange (thinly sliced)
sprigs of watercress

Method

Fry the chicken joints slowly in butter until golden-brown and tender, allowing 8–10 minutes on each side for legs and a little less for breasts. Allow to cool.

Cover each slice of bread with a lettuce leaf, place a chicken joint on top with a bacon roll alongside. Make a cut in a slice of orange, twist or curl it like a butterfly and lay it carefully on the chicken; tuck a sprig of watercress between the chicken and bacon.

Hard-boiled egg and caviar

wholemeal bread (sliced and buttered)

For each slice of bread use:
1 lettuce leaf
4 slices of hard-boiled egg
4 slices of tomato
1 tablespoon mayonnaise
1 tablespoon Danish caviar
tomato snippets

Method

Cover each slice of bread with a lettuce leaf and arrange the slices of egg with the tomato on the lettuce. Spoon the mayonnaise down the centre and top this with the caviar. Scatter on the tomato snippets.

Liver pâté

1 slice liver pâté for each slice of bread
rye bread (thinly sliced and well buttered)
French mustard
1 cocktail sausage for each slice of bread
tomatoes (sliced)
gherkins

Method

Spread the buttered bread with a little of the mustard and then cover with a slice of liver pâté. Garnish each sandwich with a cocktail sausage (cut in half), two slices of tomato and a gherkin, cut into a fan shape.

On the large tray are sandwiches made from recipes on these pages

Danish raspberry shortcake

1 lb raspberries (frozen, or fresh in season)
3 tablespoons redcurrant glaze
1 small carton (about 3 fl oz) of double cream (whipped) – optional

For pastry
4 oz plain flour
3 oz butter
1¼ oz icing sugar (sifted)
1 egg yolk
2–3 drops of vanilla essence

We have found that if you buy raspberries frozen *without* sugar which are packed in a *rigid* container, and leave them to thaw overnight at refrigerated temperature, they will be quite dry and will look and taste like the freshly picked fruit, if you cannot find these, you should use a firmer fruit such as pineapple or apricots with an apricot glaze. Do not use canned raspberries as they are too soft to glaze.

Brush the glaze thickly over the raspberries and leave it to set before decorating

Method

First prepare pastry: sift the flour on to a board or marble slab, make a well in the middle and put all the other ingredients in this. Work them to a smooth paste with the fingertips of one hand, drawing in the flour gradually; then chill pastry in refrigerator for 30 minutes.

Meanwhile set oven at 375°F or Mark 5.

Roll or pat out pastry to a round, ¼ inch thick and 7–8 inches in diameter, slide it on to a baking sheet and bake blind in pre-set oven for about 15–20 minutes. The pastry should not brown but look like shortbread.

When pastry is cool, cover it with the raspberries and brush with redcurrant glaze. When

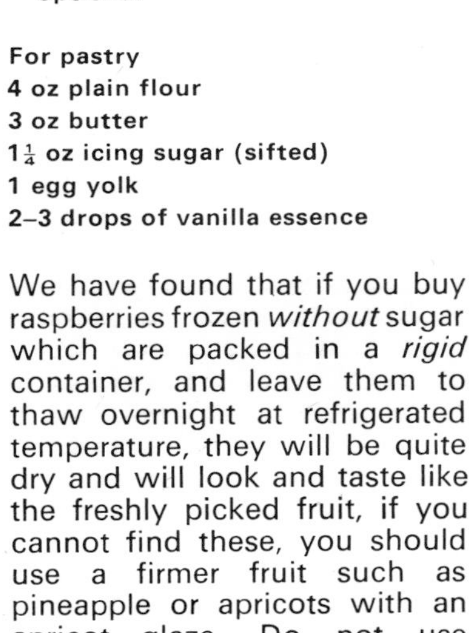

quite cold, decorate shortcake with whipped cream or serve it separately.

Watchpoint If you choose canned fruit, it is wise to make double the quantity of glaze and brush the shortcake with a thin coating of this, then leave it to set before arranging drained fruit on top. This will prevent juices from the canned fruit on top soaking into the pastry. Glaze a second time on top of the fruit.

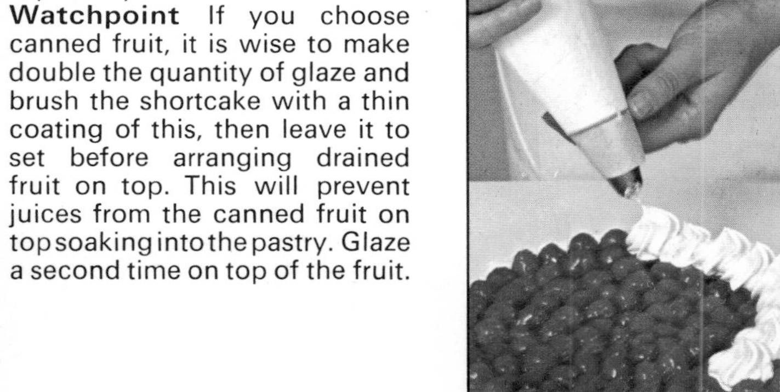

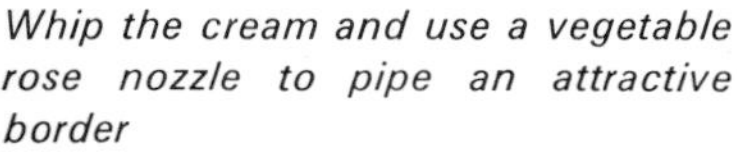

Whip the cream and use a vegetable rose nozzle to pipe an attractive border

Peasant girl in a veil

2 lb ripe red plums
4 oz sugar
8 tablespoons white breadcrumbs
2 oz butter
a little caster sugar
$\frac{1}{4}$ pint double cream
1 egg white

Method

Set oven at 350°F or Mark 4.

Wipe the plums, split and remove stones. Lay plums in a dish and sprinkle thickly with sugar, cover and cook in pre-set moderate oven for 35–40 minutes until soft. Allow to cool.

Fry the crumbs in butter until brown, scattering with a little caster sugar. Lay the plums, free from juice, in a glass dish or bowl in layers with the crumbs. Whisk the cream until partially whipped. Whisk egg white until it stands in peaks and fold into the cream. Spread over plums and chill before serving.

Swedish apple charlotte

2 lb cooking apples
4 tablespoons granulated sugar
1 cup fresh breadcrumbs
4 oz butter

For apricot sauce
4 tablespoons apricot jam
$\frac{1}{3}$ pint water
grated rind and juice of 1 lemon
1 teaspoon arrowroot
cream (optional)

Charlotte tin ($1\frac{1}{2}$ pint capacity), or 6-inch diameter soufflé dish

Method

Cook apples to a purée with granulated sugar.

Fry the breadcrumbs in butter until crisp and golden-brown. Fill a charlotte tin or soufflé dish with alternate layers of fried crumbs and apple purée. Begin and end with crumbs. Bake for about 30 minutes in an oven at 375°F or Mark 5.

To make apricot sauce: bring jam, water, lemon rind and juice slowly to the boil, then thicken with a little arrowroot slaked with cold water, and boil sauce until it is clear. Strain before using.

Turn out the apple charlotte for serving and hand round the apricot sauce or cream.

The New World

The continents of Australasia and America provide luxuriant variations on European food. Fish are bigger, shellfish more plentiful; steaks and hams are cheaper and even the fruit seems to ripen to a more juicy fullness. Add to the variety of foods the wide heritage of cooking traditions carried to the new world by emigrants from the old world and the result is a diet of richness and plenty.

Each of the countries represented in this section has its own specialities. Australia is particularly renowned for its oyster soup and carpet bag steaks. In Europe we use canned oysters to make these dishes, but at home only the real thing will do. The rivers of New Zealand supply trout for baking and stuffing. Canada has plentiful supplies of all good foods, but part of its national heritage is the maple tree from which the sap is extracted and boiled to make the maple syrup which accompanies all Canadian pancakes. The USA covers such a wide area and wide range of climates that almost any dish could be said to be typical of somewhere, but the fried dishes of the southern states, fried hamburgers with buns and onions, angel cake and brownies are known throughout the world.

Oyster soup

12 oysters, or 1 can of oysters
2 oz butter
2 shallots (finely chopped)
$\frac{1}{2}$ teaspoon paprika pepper
pinch of ground mace
1 tablespoon cornflour
1 can (about 12 oz) evaporated milk
$\frac{3}{4}$ pint milk
salt and pepper

Method

Melt the butter and add the shallots, cover and cook slowly until golden. Add the paprika and mace, cook for 1 minute then blend in the cornflour, evaporated milk and milk. Season and stir until boiling, then simmer for 3–4 minutes. Remove the oysters from their shells, and add them, with any liquid (or canned ones with their juice), to the pan. Reheat carefully without boiling.

Oysters
Nowadays in Great Britain oysters are so expensive that fresh ones are considered a delicacy only to be eaten raw. This has not always been the case: in 1712 the best oysters sold for 15p a barrel and the poor bought them from barrows in the streets. After about 1850 exploitation of the oyster beds and disease combined to raise the price of European oysters. In Australia, however, they are not too costly to be used in soup.

Carpet bag steak

This recipe is a speciality from New South Wales, particularly Sydney, where the oysters are really first class. For barbecue parties a thick rump steak sufficient for 4–6 people is usually used, but for a dinner party dry fried fillet steaks are the rule. Rump steak cut $1\frac{1}{2}$ inches thick will require 12–16 oysters. For fillet steak, if the oysters are very small use 2 per steak; if large, 1 oyster would be sufficient.

For rump steak cut a pocket in the steak, fill with the oysters and then sprinkle with a few drops of lemon juice and grind on a little pepper from the mill. Secure with poultry pins or sew up with fine string and a trussing needle. Brush with a little melted butter and cook for 7–10 minutes on each side.

To serve, melt $\frac{1}{2}$–$\frac{3}{4}$ oz butter in a small pan and when it is nut-brown pour in the juice of $\frac{1}{2}$ lemon, season with salt and pepper and 1 teaspoon of chopped parsley. Pour foaming over the steak and serve at once.

For fillet steak cut a pocket in the same way and fill with 1–2 oysters. Dry fry these steaks and after cooking wipe out the pan and prepare and serve the butter sauce as described above.

Steak Diane

4 minute steaks
$1\frac{1}{2}$ oz butter
2 shallots, or spring onions (very finely chopped)
2 tablespoons brandy, or $2\frac{1}{2}$ fl oz Marsala
1 tablespoon Worcestershire sauce
scant $\frac{1}{4}$ pint demi-glace sauce
2–3 tablespoons freshly made tomato sauce (see page 49)
1 tablespoon chopped parsley

This famous dish originated at a well-known restaurant in Australia. It is always prepared by the head waiter at the table and to be really delicious the waiter must be able to call on a first class demi-glace sauce and tomato sauce from the main kitchen.

Unless the home cook has about $\frac{1}{4}$ pint of good demi-glace sauce in the refrigerator or freezer, and 2 tablespoons of a freshly made tomato sauce, this recipe is extremely difficult to prepare at home with the same ease and speed that it is produced in a good restaurant.

Method

Drop half the butter into a large frying pan, or chafing dish, and when hot and foaming put in the minute steaks and cook quickly until coloured on each side. (If the steaks are well cut and batted out, they should be sufficiently cooked in 1 minute.)

Add the shallots (or spring onions), pour the brandy (or Marsala) into the pan, set alight and allow the flames to burn out. Add the Worcestershire sauce and follow it with the brown and tomato sauces. Let all simmer really well together, then add the remaining butter (in small pieces) and the parsley. Shake the pan to blend in and serve at once.

A typical Australian vegetable to serve with this would be baked squash. We suggest that you serve it with courgettes au beurre and small new potatoes plainly boiled and then tossed in butter and chopped parsley.
Note: 'squash' here refers to the fruit produced on a vine by plants belonging to the gourd and pumpkin families. Marrow is one variety of squash, but it is not suitable for baking in this way as are some squash.

Barossa chicken

$3\frac{1}{2}$ lb roasting chicken
$1\frac{1}{2}$–2 oz butter
1 wineglass white wine
1 lettuce (shredded)
4 oz almonds (blanched and split)
2 tablespoons olive oil
$\frac{1}{2}$ lb muscat grapes
squeeze of lemon juice
salt and pepper

For dressing
1 wineglass white wine
juice of $\frac{1}{2}$ lemon
about $\frac{1}{4}$ pint olive oil
1 tablespoon mixed chopped herbs (parsley, mint and chives)

This recipe was called Barossa after the name of an Australian vineyard.

Method

Set oven at 400°F or Mark 6. Roast the chicken for about 1 hour with the butter and white wine. Reserve any juice from roasting chicken. Leave chicken to get quite cold, then joint it and arrange on the shredded lettuce on a serving dish.

Fry the almonds in the oil until brown, drain and salt them lightly. Peel and pip the grapes, put them in a small basin or tea cup, sprinkle with a little lemon juice to prevent discolouration, cover with greaseproof paper.

To make the dressing: reduce the wine to half quantity, then take it off heat. Mix the wine with the rest of the ingredients, seasoning and juice reserved from roasting the chicken, well skimmed of any fat. Add the grapes, and spoon this dressing over the chicken; then scatter over the almonds.

Lamingtons

3-egg quantity of Victoria sponge mixture, or 3-egg quantity of genoese pastry
$\frac{1}{2}$ lb apricot glaze

For chocolate glacé icing
3 oz block chocolate
4 tablespoons water
8 oz icing sugar
few drops of vanilla essence
1 teaspoon salad oil, or $\frac{1}{4}$ oz unsalted butter
4 oz desiccated coconut

8-inch square cake tin, or swiss roll tin (8 inches by 12 inches)

These little sponge cakes can be made either with an English Victoria sandwich mixture or a French genoese pastry.

Method

Set the oven at 375°F or Mark 5. Prepare cake tin and your chosen cake mixture and bake in the pre-set oven for 20 minutes. Turn on to a wire rack and when cool trim the edges of the cake and then cut it in squares.

Heat the apricot glaze and brush each square with it; leave to set. To make glacé icing, melt chocolate in water over very gentle heat, then bring just to the boil. Cool before beating in sugar, one spoonful at a time. Add oil (or butter) and vanilla and warm slightly.

Place each piece of cake in turn on a fork, dip into the warm glacé icing and roll at once in the desiccated coconut. Return to the wire rack and leave until cool.

Curried crayfish

The following recipe could be done with cooked lobster or white crab meat, or even prawns. The quantity of sauce given here allows for $1\frac{1}{2}$ lb fish.

$1\frac{1}{2}$ lb crayfish meat (chopped)
chopped parsley
squeeze of lemon juice

For curry sauce
1 medium-size onion (sliced)
1 medium-size apple (sliced)
1 oz butter
1 dessertspoon curry powder
$\frac{1}{2}$–$\frac{3}{4}$ pint milk
1 dessertspoon chutney
1 dessertspoon sultanas
1 dessertspoon sugar
1 dessertspoon desiccated coconut
salt and pepper
2 tablespoons plain flour (mixed to a paste with 4 tablespoons milk)

Method

Sauté the slices of onion and apple in butter. Add the curry powder and cook for 2 minutes, then add the milk and all remaining curry sauce ingredients except the flour paste. When almost boiling thicken with the flour paste. Simmer for 3 minutes, then add the chopped crayfish meat, parsley and lemon juice; heat through and serve.

Stuffed fish

two $1\frac{1}{2}$ lb, or one $3\frac{1}{2}$ lb, fish
$\frac{1}{4}$ pint sherry
$\frac{1}{4}$ pint milk

For stuffing
$\frac{1}{2}$ small onion (chopped)
2 tablespoons melted butter
3 oz white breadcrumbs
$\frac{1}{2}$ teaspoon salt
pepper (ground from mill)
1 tablespoon chopped parsley
pinch of dried mixed herbs
2 tablespoons hot water

In New Zealand trout are really the finest fish and are caught in many of the lakes and rivers on both islands. This recipe is quite excellent for our own sea trout and would do for any whole, firm, round fish.

Method

Wash and dry fish very well; if it has only been cleaned through the gills by the fishmonger, slit it down the belly. Wash and clean cavity very well and dry thoroughly. Then place fish in a casserole, pour over the sherry, cover and leave in the refrigerator overnight.

Set the oven at 350°F or Mark 4. To prepare the stuffing: soften onion in butter and add it to crumbs. Add the seasoning, parsley, herbs and hot water. Place the stuffing in the fish, pour over the milk, season and bake in the pre-set moderate oven 35–40 minutes for a $3\frac{1}{2}$ lb fish or 20–25 minutes for a $1\frac{1}{2}$ lb fish. Serve hot or cold.

The marinated sea trout is stuffed before baking in milk

Below: stuffed sea trout, served with a choice of green vegetables

Pavlova

4 egg whites
$\frac{1}{4}$ teaspoon salt
8 oz caster sugar
4 teaspoons cornflour
2 teaspoons vinegar
$\frac{1}{2}$ teaspoon vanilla essence
$\frac{1}{2}$ pint double cream
a selection of fresh fruit, or canned fruit salad

9-inch diameter shallow ovenproof dish

Method

Set the oven at 275°F or Mark 1. Beat the egg whites and salt with a rotary whisk or electric mixer until stiff. Add the sugar, 1 tablespoon at a time, whisking until very stiff, then beat in the cornflour, vinegar and vanilla. Butter a shallow ovenproof dish, fill with the meringue mixture; hollow out the centre somewhat.

Bake for $1\frac{1}{4}$ hours in the slow pre-set oven. When cool fill with sweetened and flavoured cream and fresh fruit.

Note: in Australia this is served filled with a little fresh whipped cream and a lot of tropical fruit: banana, mixed with passion fruit and sometimes fresh pineapple or pawpaw. In Great Britain increase the quantity of cream to $\frac{1}{2}$ pint. To give the same authentic flavour, tropical fruit salad (canned in Australia) could be served separately.

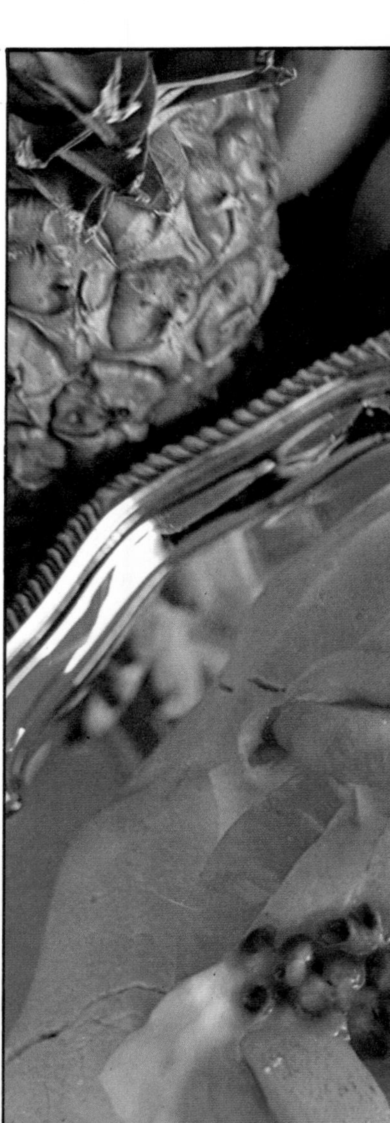

Pavlova, a meringue sweet popular in Australia and New Zealand, is served filled with whipped cream and fruit

Avocado pear and tomato ice

3 avocado pears
1 can (14 oz) tomatoes
1 clove of garlic (crushed)
$\frac{1}{2}$ teaspoon salt
2 tablespoons sugar
pared rind and juice of $\frac{1}{2}$ lemon
1 stick of celery (sliced)
1 onion (sliced)
3 sprigs of mint
Tabasco, and Worcestershire, sauce (to taste)

Ice-cream churn freezer

This dish serves 6 as a starter.

Method

Tip the canned tomatoes into a pan, add the garlic, salt, sugar, lemon rind and juice, celery and onion and stir until boiling. Press the tomatoes well, then add the sprigs of mint. Cover the pan and allow to simmer for 5–10 minutes. Remove the mint and rub the contents of the pan through a nylon sieve (leaving behind celery and onion). Allow to cool, add the Tabasco and Worcestershire sauces to taste. This mixture should be rather over-flavoured as freezing takes some out.

Chill the mixture really well then turn into a freezer and churn until firm. Allow to ripen for 1 hour before serving

For serving, slightly chill the avocados, cut in half and remove the stone. Place a good scoop of the ice in the cavity.

Avocado pear with tomato ice makes a Canadian-style party starter

Nova Scotia seafood platter

4 oz Nova Scotia salmon (smoked salmon)
½ lb Alaskan king crab (white crab meat)
12 jumbo shrimps, or Mediterranean prawns, or 6 oz frozen prawns
1 packet (2 fillets) marinated herrings (sliced on the slant)
1 small head of celery
2–3 carrots
1 Webb's, or Iceberg, lettuce
1 sweet pickled cucumber
bunch of spring onions
6 black olives
6 green olives (stuffed with pimiento or anchovy)
¼ pint mayonnaise
French mustard
1 carton (5 fl oz) soured cream
2–3 tablespoons tomato ketchup
dash of Tabasco sauce
1 teaspoon grated horseradish, or 2 teaspoons horseradish cream
½ green pepper (finely chopped)
2 tablespoons finely chopped celery

For hors d'oeuvre, guests choose from the selection of fish, accompaniments and sauces.

Method

Wash and trim the celery and carrots and cut both into even-size sticks about the length of your little finger and half as thick. Wash and dry the lettuce. Slice the pickled cucumber and prepare spring onions.

Place the crisp lettuce leaves on a large platter and arrange the fish in groups on them. Garnish with the celery and carrot sticks, cucumber, spring onions and olives.

Mix the mayonnaise with mustard to taste, and serve in a small bowl for dunking. Put the soured cream in a second small bowl. Mix the tomato ketchup with all the remaining ingredients (this sauce should be fairly hot with Tabasco and horseradish) and serve in the same way as the mustard mayonnaise.

Baked ham

4 lb joint of gammon
1 onion
1 carrot
1 stick of celery
bouquet garni
6 peppercorns

For glaze
4 tablespoons golden syrup
4 oz brown sugar
1 teaspoon English mustard
white wine vinegar (to moisten)
12 cloves

Method

Soak the joint for 4 hours in cold water to cover. Throw away the water, cover the joint again with fresh cold water, bring slowly to the boil and skim well. Add the vegetables, bouquet garni and peppercorns; cover and simmer gently for 2 hours. Take up the joint, remove the skin and score the fat in diamonds with a sharp knife.

Set the oven at 350°F or Mark 4. Place the joint in a baking tin and brush over it with warmed golden syrup. Mix the brown sugar and dry mustard with enough vinegar to moisten and spread over the surface of the ham. Stick with the cloves and bake in the pre-set moderate oven until golden-brown (about 20 minutes). Serve hot with raisin sauce.

Raisin sauce

4 oz seeded raisins (cut in small pieces)
8 oz granulated sugar
$\frac{1}{4}$ pint water
1 oz butter
1 tablespoon Worcestershire sauce
3 tablespoons wine vinegar
a few drops of Tabasco sauce
salt and pepper
small pinch of ground mace
4 oz redcurrant jelly

Method

Dissolve the sugar in the water and boil steadily for 5 minutes. Add all the other ingredients and simmer gently until the redcurrant jelly has dissolved. Served this hot with the ham.

1
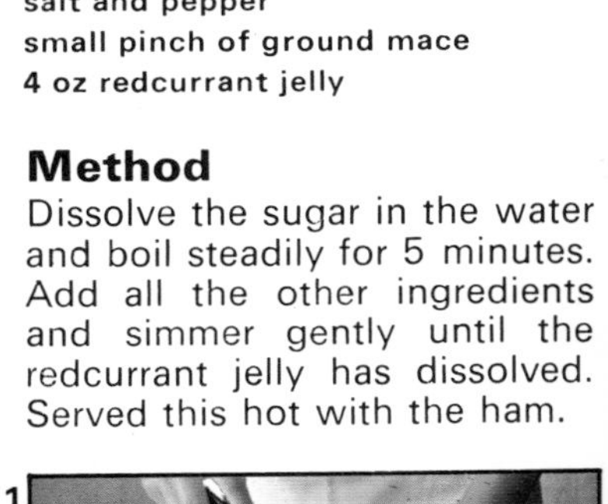

2

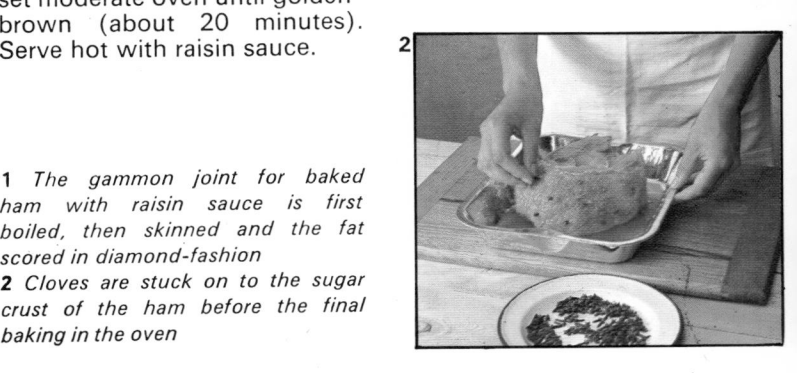

1 *The gammon joint for baked ham with raisin sauce is first boiled, then skinned and the fat scored in diamond-fashion*

2 *Cloves are stuck on to the sugar crust of the ham before the final baking in the oven*

Game casserole

2 lb venison, or moose (a piece cut from the shoulder blade, saddle or haunch of venison)
1 teaspoon salt
$\frac{1}{4}$ teaspoon pepper (ground from mill)
1 bayleaf (crushed or cut in small pieces)
$\frac{1}{2}$ teaspoon rosemary
$\frac{1}{2}$–$\frac{3}{4}$ pint milk
$\frac{1}{2}$ lb pickled belly pork
1 oz plain flour
1 teaspoon paprika pepper
about 1 tablespoon salad oil
1 oz butter
2 large onions (finely sliced)
1 pint jellied stock
2 wineglasses red wine
1 small carton ($2\frac{1}{2}$ fl oz) soured cream
juice of $\frac{1}{2}$ small lemon

Method

If using moose cut away any fat. Cut the moose or venison into 1-inch cubes, place in a casserole or bowl, sprinkle with the seasonings and herbs and pour over the milk. Cover and leave in the refrigerator for 24 hours, turning occasionally.

Cover the pork with cold water and bring to the boil, drain and cut into dice. Drain the milk off the meat, mix the flour and paprika together and dust enough over the meat to coat each piece and to dry the surface.

Heat the salad oil, add the pork and cook until the dice are golden-brown on all sides. Add the butter to the pan and, when foaming, put in the meat a few pieces at a time and cook fairly quickly until pieces are lightly coloured. Remove meat from the fat with a draining spoon. When all the meat has been browned in this way and removed from the pan, add the onions, lower the heat and cook slowly, stirring from time to time, until golden-brown.

Add the stock and wine and bring to the boil. Return the meat to the pan, cover and simmer very gently for about 2 hours or until tender. This could be done on top of the stove or in the oven, set at 325°F or Mark 3.

Mix any remaining flour and paprika with the soured cream and lemon juice and add to the casserole. Stir until mixture thickens and taste for seasoning. Serve with creamed potatoes.

Lemon cheese tart

1 packet (8 oz) wheatmeal biscuits
1 oz caster sugar
2 oz butter (melted)

For filling
8 oz Philadelphia cream cheese
4 oz lemon curd
3 egg yolks

8-inch diameter flan ring, or pie plate

Method

Crush the biscuits with a rolling pin and mix with the sugar. Mix two-thirds of this into the melted butter, press into the flan ring (or pie plate) and chill well.

Set the oven at 350°F or Mark 4. Mix the cream cheese and lemon curd together, stir and add the egg yolks. Pour the mixture into the chilled pastry shell. Sprinkle with the reserved crumbs and bake for 20 minutes in the pre-set oven. Cool and chill again before serving.

Lemon curd

To make 1 lb lemon curd, put 8 oz caster sugar, 4 oz unsalted butter, the grated rind and strained juice of 2 large lemons and 3 well-beaten eggs into an enamel pan (or stone jam jar) standing in boiling water. Stir gently over low heat until mixture is thick (do not let it boil or it will curdle), then pour immediately into clean, dry jars and cover tightly. Lemon curd will keep for several weeks if stored in a cool place.

Raisin pie

For shortcrust pastry
8 oz plain flour
pinch of salt
2 oz shortening
4 oz butter
3–4 tablespoons cold water

For filling
8 oz seedless raisins
$\frac{3}{4}$ pint water
4 oz granulated sugar
$\frac{3}{4}$ oz plain flour
pinch of salt
2 drops of vanilla essence
$\frac{1}{2}$ oz butter
juice of $\frac{1}{4}$ lemon

To finish
water, or 1 egg white (lightly beaten)
caster sugar

8–9 inch diameter pie plate

Method

Prepare the pastry, adding enough water to make the dough cling together; chill well.

To prepare the filling: simmer the raisins and water together for 10 minutes. Mix the sugar, flour and salt together and carefully stir in the raisin mixture. Add the vanilla, butter and lemon juice and allow to cool.

Set the oven at 425°F or Mark 7. Roll out half the pastry and line into the pie plate. Fill the pie with the cooled raisin mixture and cover with the remaining pastry. Seal the edges well, flute and then make two or three slits in the top crust. Brush with the water (or egg white), dust with the sugar and bake in the pre-set oven for 15 minutes or until the top is golden. Cover with greaseproof paper, reduce heat to 350°F or Mark 4 and bake for 25–30 minutes more.

Pancakes with maple syrup

6 oz superfine flour (sifted)
$1\frac{1}{2}$ teaspoons baking powder
1 teaspoon caster sugar
large pinch of salt
1 egg
7–8 fl oz milk
1 oz butter (melted)

In Canada these are eaten for breakfast with crispy fried bacon. This quantity makes 12–16 pancakes.

Method

Sift the flour into a mixing bowl with the baking powder, sugar and salt. Beat the egg very well, add the milk to it and then add this mixture to the flour with the melted butter and beat well until really smooth. (A rotary beater is best for this.) Beat for at least 3 minutes until bubbles are breaking freely over the surface.

While batter is being made heat a heavy girdle until a few drops of cold water sprinkled on it will literally dance about.

Fry the pancakes until golden-brown. If the heat is right, the pancakes will brown immediately.

Note: the pancakes can be made thick or thin just as you like and it is quite easy to adjust the batter by adding a little extra milk if you like your pancakes really thin.

Turn the pancakes as soon as they are puffy and full of bubbles but it is most important, if the pancakes are to be really light, that you turn them before these bubbles break.

Serve them in stacks of 3–4 per person with pats of unsalted butter and a jug of maple syrup.

Butter tarts

For rich shortcrust pastry
8 oz plain flour
6 oz butter
1 oz shortening
2–3 tablespoons milk (to mix)

For filling
2–3 oz currants, or seedless raisins
2 oz butter
4 oz soft brown sugar
10 oz golden syrup
2–3 drops of vanilla essence
2 eggs

6 individual ovenproof fluted dishes (4–5 inches diameter)

The proportion of butter to flour in this recipe is correct for the more absorbent North American flour. If using English flour, use only 4–5 oz butter.

Method

Make up the pastry, line into the dishes and bake blind.

Turn the oven to 375°F or Mark 5.

To prepare the filling: pour boiling water on to the currants (or raisins). Cream the butter, sugar and syrup together and add the vanilla. Break the eggs with a fork – but do not beat – and stir into the syrup mixture. Drain the currants (or raisins) and dry with absorbent paper. Put the fruit at the bottom of the cooked pastry cases and pour on the syrup mixture. Bake for 10–15 minutes in the pre-set oven.

Split pea soup

1 lb beef shin bone (cut in 2-inch lengths)
4 pints cold water
$\frac{1}{2}$ lb leg of beef (shin)
3 oz split peas
2 onions (finely sliced)
2 carrots (finely sliced)
2 sticks of celery (finely sliced)
large bouquet garni (containing a good sprig of thyme)
$\frac{1}{2}$ teaspoon salt
pepper (ground from mill)

Method

Cover the beef bones with the water, bring slowly to the boil and skim well. Cut the leg of beef in very small shreds, add to the pan and allow to simmer gently for 1 hour. Add the split peas and continue cooking for about 50 minutes. Now add all the vegetables, bouquet garni and seasoning and continue cooking until the root vegetables are quite tender, allowing a further 40–50 minutes for this. Taste for seasoning, remove bouquet garni and serve.

Lamb pot roast

$4\frac{1}{2}$ lb leg of lamb
2 tablespoons salad oil
salt and pepper
a little cornflour

Method

Heat the salad oil in a large heavy pan. Put in the leg of lamb and cook gently, turning until all sides are nicely coloured. This should take about 30 minutes. Season lightly, put in 2 tablespoons of water, cover tightly and cook very gently for $1\frac{3}{4}$–2 hours.

For serving take up the lamb, tip $\frac{1}{2}$ pint of hot water into the pan and boil up well. Season to taste and thicken the gravy with a little cornflour mixed to a paste with water. Serve with vegetables separately.

Beef pot roast

Topside of beef is cooked in a casserole the same way as the lamb but after the first hour's cooking a dozen button onions and 6–8 even-size potatoes are added to the pan. These brown quite nicely with the meat and are dished up around it.

Curried brawn

- **1 calves foot (split), or 2 lb cow heel**
- **1 lb tripe**
- **4 pints water**
- **½ teaspoon salt**
- **1 large onion (peeled)**
- **½ lb shin of beef**
- **1 rasher of bacon**
- **½ clove of garlic (chopped)**
- **1 teaspoon curry powder**
- **½ teaspoon dried thyme**
- **1 clove**

Method

Wash the calves foot (or cow heel) and tripe and put into a large pan. Cover with the water, add the salt and bring slowly to the boil. Skim well and simmer gently for 2 hours. Add the onion and beef and continue cooking until tender (about 1 hour).

Meanwhile remove the rind from the bacon, cut in small pieces, put in a small pan and cook gently until the fat begins to run. Add the garlic and curry powder and fry gently for about 5 minutes. Add a teacupful of the liquid from the large pan and the thyme and clove; cover and simmer for about 10 minutes.

Remove the tripe and piece of beef from the saucepan and cut into small pieces. Lift out the calves foot, remove the bone and cut the jellied meat in the same-size pieces as the beef and tripe. Put all this meat into the curry saucepan, add an extra cup of liquid and simmer very gently for about 5 minutes. Turn this mixture into 1–2 pudding basins, adding enough of the liquid from the saucepan to cover. Leave in a cool place to set.

This brawn should be served with salad, preferably freshly picked from the garden. After washing, serve lettuce quite plain in one bowl and tomatoes in another.

Prawns Alabama

4–6 Dublin Bay prawns per person, or 10 oz frozen prawns
lemon juice
black pepper (ground from mill)
lettuce leaves
paprika pepper

For Alabama sauce
4 fl oz tomato sauce (see page 49), or tomato ketchup, or tomato juice
$\frac{1}{2}$ pint very thick mayonnaise
1 small head of celery (chopped), or $\frac{1}{2}$ cucumber (finely diced)
1 small, or $\frac{1}{2}$ large, green pepper (seeds removed and flesh chopped)
1 rounded tablespoon freshly grated horseradish
1 clove of garlic (crushed with $\frac{1}{4}$ teaspoon salt)
2–3 tablespoons double cream
few drops of Tabasco sauce

Alabama sauce can also be used as a dip for a cocktail party.

Method

Shell the Dublin Bay prawns, or thaw out frozen prawns. Sprinkle over a little lemon juice and black pepper, then cover and leave to marinate while preparing the sauce.

Add tomato sauce (or ketchup or juice) to mayonnaise, whisking it well. If using cucumber, sprinkle with salt and leave for 15 minutes, then drain thoroughly. Add it, or celery, to sauce, with chopped pepper, horseradish, garlic, double cream and Tabasco. The sauce must be quite spicy and piquant – add more seasoning if necessary.

Arrange the drained prawns on the lettuce leaves on individual plates and coat with 2–3 tablespoons of sauce. Dust with paprika and serve chilled. If you wish, shred the lettuce and put in coupe glasses with the prawns and sauce on top.

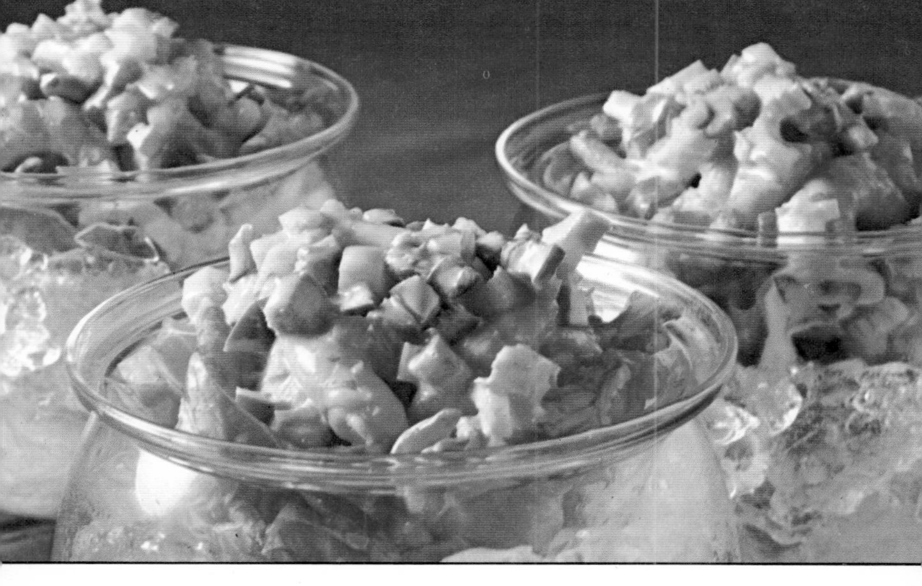

Fried (or grilled) chicken
with sweetcorn fritters

6–8 chicken joints (breast and wing joints), or 2 young chickens
2 tablespoons seasoned plain flour
1 egg (beaten)
1 tablespoon oil
1 cup of fresh white breadcrumbs
4 oz clarified butter

For sweetcorn fritters
1 cup of cooked frozen, or canned, sweetcorn kernels
2 eggs
salt and pepper
pinch of sugar
1 teaspoon baking powder
$\frac{1}{2}$–1 cup of fresh breadcrumbs
oil (for frying)

For sauce
1 oz butter
1 rounded tablespoon plain flour
$\frac{3}{4}$ cup of chicken stock, or bouillon cube with water
salt and pepper
1 dessertspoon grated horseradish
squeeze of lemon juice
5 tablespoons single cream

For garnish
8 rashers of streaky bacon

Method

If using whole chickens, joint and trim them. Roll in the seasoned flour.

Brush chicken joints with the beaten egg (to which the oil has been added), roll in the breadcrumbs and press them on firmly with a palette knife.

Watchpoint Adding oil to a beaten egg before egging and crumbing chicken or veal helps to keep the meat moist.

To prepare fritters: separate the eggs, beat yolks well with the seasoning and sugar and then add the sweetcorn. Beat egg whites until stiff and fold into the sweetcorn with the baking powder and enough breadcrumbs to bring the mixture to a dropping consistency.

Heat the oil (enough to give a depth of $\frac{1}{4}$ inch in the frying pan), drop in sweetcorn mixture, a dessertspoon at a time, and fry until golden-brown on one side before turning and browning on the other side. Then lift out with a draining spoon, leave on crumpled absorbent paper in warming drawer or at bottom of oven.

To prepare sauce: melt the butter in a pan, stir in flour and cook gently until a pale straw colour; remove from the heat, blend in stock and season to taste. Stir over gentle heat until boiling, simmer for 2–3 minutes, then add the horseradish, lemon juice and cream. Keep warm.

To fry chicken: heat the clarified butter in a large frying pan, arrange pieces of chicken in this and fry gently, turning occasionally so that they are well browned on all sides.

If you prefer to grill the joints, baste well with heated, clarified butter before and during cooking. When cooked, arrange in a hot dish with fritters and keep warm.

To garnish: remove rind from the bacon, fry or grill and arrange round the chicken. Serve the sauce separately.

A helping of fried chicken with sweetcorn fritters, bacon and green salad with fresh pineapple

Broadway chicken pie

3 lb roasting chicken
1 onion (finely chopped)
1 oz butter
4–5 tablespoons long grain rice (boiled)
½ lb spinach (blanched and chopped)
2 small eggs (beaten)
about ½ pint chicken stock
kneaded butter, or slaked arrowroot (for thickening)
1 glass Madeira, or sherry
¼ lb streaky bacon rashers
4–6 oz mushrooms (whole, or quartered)
½ lb good tomatoes (skinned, quartered and seeds removed)
8 oz quantity of flaky pastry

Deep 7–8 inch long pie dish (1½ pints capacity)

Method

Bone out the chicken. Soften the onion in the butter. Turn into a bowl with the rice and spinach. Bind with half the beaten egg mixture. Fill this farce into chicken and sew up.

Braise chicken in a large pan or flameproof casserole for 45–50 minutes in a little good stock. Cool it a little, reduce stock well and thicken it slightly with kneaded butter (or arrowroot), after adding the Madeira (or sherry).

Cut chicken into slices; lay in a dish with bacon, mushrooms and tomatoes. Moisten chicken slices with the stock, cover with the flaky pastry, decorate well, brush with beaten egg and bake in a hot oven at 400°F or Mark 6 or 35–40 minutes.

Maryland tomatoes

4–5 large tomatoes
salt and pepper
2–3 tablespoons browned crumbs
2 tablespoons demerara sugar
melted butter

This dish should be served as a starter.

Method

Cut tomatoes in two, lay them in a buttered ovenproof dish, season and cook in a moderate oven at 350°F or Mark 4 for 7–10 minutes.

Mix the crumbs and sugar together and moisten with the melted butter. Sprinkle this mixture over the tomatoes and return to a hot oven at 400°F or Mark 6 for 5–10 minutes, or quickly brown under the grill.

American lamb hot pot

1 large leg of lamb, or 2 small ones (the joints must be large enough to give 3 lb meat when cut from the bone)
4 tablespoons plain flour (sifted with 1 teaspoon salt and $\frac{1}{2}$ teaspoon pepper)
2 tablespoons dripping
4 large onions (finely chopped)
4 tablespoons tomato purée
4 pints jellied stock
$\frac{1}{2}$ lb mushrooms
3–4 large potatoes
2 oz butter
grated Parmesan cheese (for dusting)

Method

Cut the meat from the bone into 1–1$\frac{1}{2}$ inch cubes. (Perhaps the butcher will do this; if so, remember to ask him for the bone, from which you can make your stock.) Set the oven at 325°F or Mark 3.

Roll the meat in the sifted flour, heat the dripping in a large flameproof casserole and, when hot, fry the meat until well sealed and golden-brown on all sides.

Watchpoint Do not put in more meat than would cover the bottom of the casserole at once; for this quantity you will have to fry the meat in rotation.

When all the meat is well coloured, add the finely chopped onions to the pan, cover and lower the heat. Leave to cook until the onion has lost its hard white look and is well softened. Shake the pan and stir from time to time. Work in the tomato purée and the stock and bring to the boil. Add a little extra salt and pepper if necessary, then cover the pan tightly and cook in the pre-set oven for 1$\frac{1}{2}$–2 hours.

Meanwhile, wash, trim and quarter mushrooms, add them to hot pot at end of cooking time and return to oven for another 10–15 minutes.

This dish may be prepared as far as this the day before and turned into a large mixing bowl to allow the meat to cool quickly, or into open casseroles, or gratin dishes, ready for reheating.

The following day scrub the potatoes and steam, or boil, in their skins until tender. Peel while still hot, holding each potato in a tea cloth to prevent burning fingers, and cut into $\frac{1}{2}$-inch slices. Arrange these overlapping to form a cover to the meat. Brush the potatoes with melted butter, dust with a very little Parmesan cheese and bake in a pre-set oven, at 375°F or Mark 5, for 30 minutes, until the potatoes are crusty and brown.

Boston baked beans

- 1 lb dried pea beans
- 2 pints water
- 2 teaspoons dry mustard
- $\frac{1}{4}$ teaspoon black, or white, pepper
- 1 tablespoon salt
- 3 medium-size onions (quartered)
- 1 tablespoon black treacle
- 1 tablespoon golden syrup
- 2 oz soft brown sugar
- $\frac{1}{2}$ lb salt belly pork

Method

Pick over and wash the beans in several changes of water, then soak overnight in 1 pint of the measured water. Mix the mustard, pepper and salt with 1 pint water in a large casserole or marmite and tip in the beans with their soaking liquor. Quarter the onion and add to the casserole with the treacle, syrup and brown sugar. Cover and put in a slow oven to bake at 250°F or Mark $\frac{1}{2}$ for 6–8 hours.

Soak the pork in cold water for 1 hour, then blanch for 10 minutes. Remove the skin, cut into lardons, add to casserole and continue cooking for about 1 hour or until the meat is very tender.

If necessary, add extra water at the same time as the pork. Remove the lid of casserole for last 30 minutes.

Hamburgers

1½ lb finely ground hamburger mince, or 1½ lb blade bone, steak, or a cut from the aitch-bone (mince it yourself)
6 tablespoons fresh breadcrumbs
¼ teaspoon dried thyme
½ teaspoon salt
pepper (ground from mill)
1 egg (beaten)

Method

Mix the breadcrumbs, thyme and seasoning with the mince, then add the beaten egg slowly and work together very well. Shape into flat cakes about ½ inch thick and the same diameter as the buns (they will then need only 3–4 minutes' frying or grilling on each side).

For serving from the kitchen the buns should be split and hot hamburgers put in the centre. At the table the bun's 'hat' is removed and the accompaniments added as desired.

Hamburger bun

2 lb plain flour
1 teaspoon salt
1 pint skimmed milk
1 oz yeast
4 oz butter
2 tablespoons caster sugar
little milk (to finish)

This quantity makes 30–40 buns.

Method

Sift the flour with the salt into a mixing bowl. Warm the milk to blood heat, add the yeast, butter and sugar, and stir until dissolved. Pour mixture at once into the centre of the flour and mix to a smooth dough. Put the dough into a greased bowl, cover with a damp cloth and set to rise in a warm place for 1 hour, or until double in bulk.

Turn the dough on to a floured board, divide into equal portions and knead into small balls. Flatten these with the palm of your hand, set them on a greased and floured baking sheet and prove for 10 minutes. Brush the tops with milk and cook for 15–20 minutes in a pre-set oven, 425°F or Mark 7.

While still hot rub the top of each bun with buttery paper.

Accompaniments

Bowl of crisp lettuce leaves.
Slices of tomato.
Very thin slices of raw Spanish onion.
Radish roses.
Bowls of : mayonnaise ; tomato chutney ; French mustard ; hot English mustard ; dill cucumbers ; coarsely chopped beetroot mixed with a little horse-radish cream ; corn, or green pepper relish.

Spicy tomato soup

Serve mugs of steaming tomato soup, using the old-fashioned type from a can, but spiced by adding the thinly pared rind of 1 orange to every can of soup while heating. If the rind is taken off in a long piece with a potato peeler, it is quite easy to remove from the soup before serving. Put a teaspoon of whipped cream on the top of each helping and dust with grated nutmeg.

Hamburgers continued

A party can be shaped around the cooking and eating of hamburgers. Home-made rolls are baked in advance, and the hamburger steak minced and shaped ready for frying. Large bowls of relishes should be provided with a selection of salads and sauces. The idea is that the guests will fill buns with hamburgers as they are fried, and as many of the relishes, salads and sauces as they like.

Chicken and pineapple salad

1 large boiling fowl, or (if preferred) 2 roasting chickens (4 lb each)
2 fresh pineapples
salt
pepper (ground from mill)
1 onion (quartered)
1 carrot (quartered)
bouquet garni
1 teaspoon sugar
2 tablespoons white wine vinegar
6 tablespoons salad oil
1 tablespoon chopped parsley
1 tablespoon chopped mint
1 bunch of watercress (to garnish)

This dish should be completed at least 2 hours before serving to give the chicken meat a chance to absorb the flavour of the pineapple dressing.

Method

Put the chicken in a large saucepan with enough water to cover. (If using roasting chickens, water should only cover legs and thighs.) Bring slowly to the boil, add the seasoning, vegetables and bouquet garni; simmer gently until quite tender. Allow about $1\frac{1}{2}$–2 hours for boiling fowl but only 50–60 minutes for roasting chicken. Leave to cool in the liquid.

Peel and slice the pineapples, cut each slice in half and stamp out the core with a small plain cutter. Mix salt, pepper, and sugar with the vinegar and whisk in the oil. Remove the skin from the chicken, cut the meat into even-size pieces and arrange on a serving dish.

Cover the chicken with the sliced pineapple, add the herbs to the dressing, whisk again and spoon over the pineapple and chicken. Garnish with watercress just before serving.

Coleslaw salad

1 small hard white, or Dutch, cabbage
¼ pint boiled dressing, or less of French dressing
salt and pepper
1 dessert apple, Cox's or Jonathan
grated carrot (optional)
paprika pepper, or parsley (chopped)

Method

Cut cabbage into four, trim away hard stalk, then slice into thin strips. Put in a mixing bowl, add the boiled or French dressing and extra seasoning to taste. Thoroughly coat every piece of cabbage, then add apple (cored and sliced but not peeled), and grated carrot. Mix well, cover and leave for 2–3 hours before serving. Pile in a dish and sprinkle with paprika or parsley.

Boiled dressing for coleslaw

1 tablespoon sugar
1 dessertspoon plain flour
1 teaspoon salt
1 dessertspoon made mustard
1 tablespoon water
¼ pint each vinegar and water (mixed)
1 egg
½ oz butter (melted)
cream, or creamy milk

Method

Mix dry ingredients together, add mustard and about 1 tablespoon of water. Add to vinegar and water and cook thoroughly for about 5 minutes. Beat egg, add butter, pour on the hot vinegar mixture and beat thoroughly.

When cold dilute with cream or milk and mix well. This dressing keeps well, covered, in a refrigerator.

American pie pastry

Pastry for the American covered pie is slightly different from shortcrust both in ingredients and method. Most recipes for American shortcrust have a high proportion of fat to flour, and usually need more liquid for binding. This is because American and Canadian flour is milled from hard wheat which is very high in gluten (the major part of the protein content of wheat flour, which gives it its elasticity), and consequently absorbs more liquid.

The following recipe is an anglicised version, but has the same short, melt-in-the-mouth texture. As the texture is very short, the pastry is not easy to handle once cooked, so serve the pie in the dish in which it is baked (a round, shallow tin or dish—pie plate—about 2–2½ inches deep). The pastry is lined into the pie plate, fruit or other mixture is poured on top, and the pie is then covered with a lid of pastry. The two recipes (right) are good examples of American pies.

Basic recipe

8 oz self-raising flour
5 oz lard, or shortening
pinch of salt
2 tablespoons cold water

Method

Place the lard or shortening in a bowl, add a good pinch of salt and the water, and cream ingredients together. Sift the flour over the softened fat and, using a round-bladed knife, cut the fat into the flour and mix to a rough dough. Chill for 30 minutes.

Turn the dough on to a floured board, knead lightly and then use for covered fruit pies.

Deep South apple pie

8 oz American pie pastry
cream

For filling
1½–2 lb cooking apples
4–5 oz sugar (brown or white)
½ teaspoon cinnamon
1 tablespoon orange marmalade
½ oz butter

7–8 inch diameter pie plate about 2 inches deep

Method

Make American pie pastry and set aside to chill. Peel, core and slice apples. Cook with the sugar and cinnamon to a thick pulp. Add marmalade and butter, beat well and continue to cook for 5 minutes longer, stirring frequently. Turn out to cool.

Divide the pastry into two. Roll out and line one piece on to the pie plate. Fill with the apple mixture, then cover with the other piece, and dry glaze. Bake for 30–40 minutes in an oven at 400°F or Mark 6.

Serve hot or cold, with plenty of thick cream.

◀ *A deep plate pie and some fillings for melt-in-the-mouth pie pastry*

Cherry pie

8 oz American pie pastry
1 egg white (for glazing)
caster sugar (for dusting)
cream

For filling
2½ cups cherries (fresh or canned, stewed and stoned)
8 fl oz cherry juice
2 rounded tablespoons caster sugar
1 tablespoon melted butter
1 tablespoon fine tapioca, or sago
2 drops of almond essence

7–8 inch diameter pie plate about 2½ inches deep

Method

Make American pie pastry and set aside to chill. Either fresh or canned Morello or red cherries (ie. not too sweet) are best for this pie. If fresh cherries are used, stone and cook in a little sugar syrup, and drain well.

Mix all the ingredients for the filling together and allow to stand for 15 minutes. Line the pastry on to the pie plate, pour in the fruit mixture and cover with the remaining pastry. Bake for 30–40 minutes in an oven at 400°F or Mark 6.

Take pie out of the oven, brush with lightly whisked egg white and dust with caster sugar. Put back into the oven, bake for a further 5–7 minutes. Serve hot or cold, with cream.

Waffles

Waffle batter (Basic recipe)

8 oz plain flour
1 teaspoon bicarbonate of soda
2 teaspoons baking powder
large pinch of salt
2 eggs
3 oz butter (melted)
$\frac{3}{4}$ pint soured milk, or buttermilk

This recipe makes about 8 waffles.

Method

First heat the waffle iron.

Sift the flour with the bicarbonate of soda, baking powder and salt into a mixing bowl, make a well in the centre and put the eggs and melted butter in this. Start adding the soured milk to the eggs and whisk gently, or mix with a wooden spoon. Draw in the flour very gradually and continue beating until mixture is quite smooth and all the milk has been added.

Pour the mixture from a small jug or spoon into the centre of the hot waffle iron, cover and leave closed until the steaming stops. The waffles should be puffed and golden-brown. Serve hot with pats of butter and a jug of maple syrup.

Cheese and bacon waffles

Fold 2 oz grated Cheddar cheese into the basic batter. Pour on to the iron and lay thin strips of streaky bacon over the batter before cooking as usual.

Nut waffles

Sprinkle 1 tablespoon roughly chopped browned walnuts over the batter as soon as it is poured on the waffle iron. Serve hot with butter and heather honey.

Bilberry waffles

Cook the waffles in the usual way, then serve them with a thickened compote of bilberries and soured cream or yoghourt.

Make compote by stewing bilberries. Thicken with 1 tablespoon arrowroot slaked with juice of 1 orange.

An electric waffle iron will solve many catering problems, especially with children in the family

Angel cake Waldorf

2 oz self-raising flour
$3\frac{1}{2}$ oz caster sugar
6 egg whites
pinch of salt
$\frac{3}{4}$ teaspoon cream of tartar
3 oz caster sugar
3 drops of vanilla essence
2 drops of almond essence

For filling
3–4 oz plain chocolate
1–2 tablespoons water
$\frac{1}{2}$ pint double cream
1 dessertspoon sugar

8–9 inch diameter angel cake tin, or cake tin with funnelled base

Method

Set oven at 375°F or Mark 5.

Sift the flour and the $3\frac{1}{2}$ oz sugar together 3 times and set aside. Place the egg whites, salt and cream of tartar in a large, perfectly dry basin and whisk with a rotary beater until foamy. Add the second portion of sugar, 2 tablespoons at a time, and the essences, and continue beating until the mixture will stand in peaks. Carefully fold in the sifted flour and sugar.

Turn the mixture into the clean, dry tin, level the surface and draw a knife through to break any air bubbles. Bake the cake in the pre-set hot oven for 30–35 minutes or until no imprint remains when a finger lightly touches the top. When the cake is done, turn it upside down on a wire rack and leave until it is quite cold and will fall easily from the tin.

To prepare the filling: melt the chocolate in the water, then allow to cool. Whip the cream until thick, add the sugar and chocolate and continue whisking until it stands in peaks.

Place the cake upside down on a plate or waxed paper. Slice a 1-inch layer off the top of the cake and put this top lid on one side. Cut down and around the inside of the cake 1 inch from the outer edge and 1 inch from the centre hole, leaving a wall of cake about 1 inch thick and a base of 1 inch at the bottom. Remove this middle 'ring' with a spoon (it can be discarded); set cake on serving plate. Completely fill the cavity with the chilled filling, replace 'lid' of cake and press gently. Serve a bowl of sugared raspberries or strawberries separately.

Cookies

American ice-box cookies are a very good idea for the busy housewife. The rich, sweet dough can be made up and rolled, then wrapped in waxed paper or foil and stored in the ice-making compartment of the refrigerator for 1–2 weeks. It may also be deep-frozen. When cookies are wanted, thin slices can be cut from the roll and quickly baked. The mixture is very soft, so do not attempt to shape it into a roll until it has been chilled. Never add extra flour to make handling easier as this really spoils the texture of the finished cookie.

Vanilla ice-box cookies

7 oz plain flour
pinch of salt
2 teaspoons baking powder
4 oz butter
8 oz caster sugar
1 egg (well beaten)
1 teaspoon vanilla essence
½ teaspoon grated lemon rind (optional)

This recipe makes about 40 cookies.

Method

Sift the flour with the salt and baking powder and set aside. Soften the butter with a wooden spoon, add the sugar a little at a time, and beat until light and creamy. Beat in the egg gradually, add the flavourings and then stir in the sifted dry ingredients. Chill the mixture until it is firm enough to handle, then shape into long rolls about 2 inches in diameter.

Cover the rolls with waxed paper and keep in the ice-making compartment of the refrigerator for about 24 hours. Cut in the thinnest possible slices and bake on a greased baking sheet in the oven, set at 400°F or Mark 6, for about 10 minutes.

Brownies

***2 oz unsweetened chocolate**
2½ oz shortening
2 eggs
8 oz sugar
3 oz plain flour
½ teaspoon baking powder
pinch of salt
4 oz shelled walnuts (roughly chopped)

8-inch square cake tin

Method

Set the oven at 350°F or Mark 4.

Cut up or grate the chocolate, put in a saucepan with the shortening and melt over gentle heat. Whisk the eggs and sugar together until light, add the chocolate mixture. Sift the flour with the baking powder and salt and stir into mixture with a wooden spoon ; stir in the nuts.

Spread into the prepared tin and bake for 30–35 minutes in the pre-set oven, or until a 'dull' crust has formed. Allow to cool slightly and cut into squares.

*If you can't get unsweetened chocolate, mix 2 oz cocoa with 5 tablespoons water and cook to a cream, and increase the quantity of shortening to 3 oz.

Brownies are often praised as being the best of American cookies

Kosher cooking

Jewish cookery has been influenced by two things. First by the dietary laws and second by the varied dispersal of the Jews. The term Kosher is applied to food that is allowed to be eaten according to ancient Jewish law. Many of the dishes spring from representations of incidents found in the Old Testament and much of the law is derived from the same source. It has been said that the dietary laws were instituted to keep the Jews a faith apart; to teach self-control and self-denial. The most important laws are :

1 Not to eat anything that 'dieth of itself or is torn whether it be fowl or beast'.
2 To eat only meat killed in the traditional way and drained of blood.
3 To eat only meat of animals who have a cloven hoof and who chew the cud.
4 To exclude birds of prey.
5 To eat only fish having scales.
6 Not to mix milk and meat.
7 To cleanse meat and fish by 'koshering' in salt and water to remove impurities.

For 2,000 years the Jews have remained faithful to these laws, but, as they have been scattered over the earth for hundreds of years, in each community they have taken a little of the local custom and taste for their own. In composing a set of Jewish recipes one is open to the protests of the many who say 'I don't make mine like that'; and many have valid arguments. The Russian-derived recipes, for instance, will vary from the Polish as will the Polish from the Spanish and so on, but basic tastes will remain the same.

Tradition plays a great part in Jewish life and the home is all-important. In celebration of festive days, services in the home – in which all the family play a part – have given rise to dishes that represent pieces of ancient history and remind the Jew of his past.

Salt beef

- 3½ lb brisket of beef (boned, or boned and rolled)
- 4 oz saltpetre
- 4 tablespoons salt
- 2 onions (sliced)
- 2 carrots (sliced)
- 1 turnip (sliced)
- 1 stick of celery (sliced)
- 1 dessertspoon salt
- 8 peppercorns
- 1 piece of bayleaf
- 1 stalk of parsley
- 1 blade of mace

Method

One week before cooking, place meat in a large bowl. Dissolve 3 oz saltpetre and 2 tablespoons salt in a little hot water and cool, then pour into the bowl. Add enough cold water to cover the meat, then cover bowl with a cloth and leave for 3 days. Discard the brine and repeat the process with the remaining saltpetre and salt. Leave for 3 days, covered, then discard the brine.

Run cold water over meat for 1 minute, then drain it well. Put prepared vegetables, seasonings and herbs and meat into a large pan with enough water to cover the joint. Cover pan, bring to the boil, then skim. Simmer meat for 1½ hours, or until it is tender and a good pink colour.

Leave meat to cool in the liquid (if serving it cold). Serve with chrane (see recipe right), sauerkraut, dill cucumber, green olives and potato balls.

Potato balls

- 1½ lb potatoes
- 1 oz margarine (butter, being made from milk, is never used with meat)
- 1 small onion (finely chopped)
- 1 egg yolk
- salt and pepper
- 1 egg (beaten)
- matzo meal (for coating)
- deep oil (for frying)

Method

Peel potatoes and boil until tender, then sieve them.

Melt the margarine and soften the onion in it over gentle heat in a covered pan. Add sieved potato, egg yolk and seasoning. Cool mixture slightly before rolling it in small balls. Coat balls with the beaten egg and roll in matzo meal. Fry in deep hot oil until golden and crisp, about 3–4 minutes. Then drain on absorbent paper and serve.

Chrane

Grate or mince 12 oz cooked beetroot and mix it with 6 tablespoons freshly grated horseradish, ¼ pint white wine vinegar, 1 teaspoon salt and a pinch of pepper. Fill in to clean jars and seal; keep for 1 week before using to develop flavour.

Gefillte fish

This recipe varies slightly from household to household, but a fairly standard one is given here. Gefillte fish is served often throughout the year, but is also a Passover favourite. The fish used in the basic mixture should be a selection of 3–4 varieties (eg. cod, haddock, halibut, bream, carp, whiting) to give a total weight of 2 lb. There are three methods of serving this chopped fish mixture – either boiled, or fried, or stuffed into a whole fish skin – recipes for which are given after the basic mixture.

Basic gefillte fish mixture

2 lb fish (skinned and filleted; skin and bone are reserved for fish stock)
2 onions
1 egg (beaten)
salt
black pepper (ground from mill)
3 tablespoons matzo meal

Method

Mince the fish and onions. Add the beaten egg and season well. Add matzo meal and mix well.

Boiled gefillte fish

basic gefillte fish mixture

For fish stock
2 onions
2 carrots
1–$1\frac{1}{2}$ pints water
bones and skin of fish
1 teaspoon salt
large pinch of pepper

Method

Roll the basic mixture into balls, measuring about 2 inches in diameter; make sure your hands are damp so that the mixture does not stick to them.

Slice one onion and one carrot, place in a pan with the water and bones and skin of fish; season. Bring liquid to the boil and simmer for 20 minutes, then strain this fish stock.

Slice the remaining onion, put into a large pan, or fish kettle, with the second carrot, also sliced. Gently place the fish balls on the bed of vegetables and pour in the fish stock at the side of the pan (to avoid breaking the fish balls). Simmer them very gently for 1–2 hours, until firm to the touch.

Lift fish balls out gently and allow them to cool. Strain the liquid and reserve carrot slices. Serve cold, on a bed of lettuce, placing a carrot slice on each fish ball. Serve the cooking liquid separately in a sauce boat.

Stuffed gefillte fish

1 carp (3–4 lb)

For fish stock
1 onion (sliced)
salt
8 peppercorns
2 pints water
stalk of parsley

For stuffing
1 medium-size onion
2 eggs (hard-boiled)
1 tablespoon sugar
white pepper
2 tablespoons oil
2 eggs (beaten)

For cooking
2 onions (sliced)
2 carrots (sliced)
½ stick of celery sliced

To garnish
chopped aspic (made from a packet of commercially prepared aspic)
bouquets of watercress

This is a rich recipe, especially suited to a festive occasion.

Method

To remove the flesh and bone from the fish, leaving the skin intact: bend the head of the fish back from the base of the head and, using a very sharp knife, work skin away from the flesh. Gently work from head to tail, keeping the head attached to the skin. Then snip bone off at head and tail with scissors. Remove flesh from the fish skin.

Put the carp bones and fish stock ingredients in a pan and simmer for 20 minutes. Strain the liquid and reserve.

To prepare stuffing: mince the carp flesh, onion and hard-boiled eggs, and mix well. Add sugar and seasoning and slowly work in the oil and enough beaten egg to bind stuffing together. (If eggs are large you may not need to use more than one.) Taking care not to break fish skin, fill it with stuffing.

Place the onions, carrots and celery in a fish kettle with the reserved fish stock. Place the stuffed fish on the vegetables

1 Starting to skin the carp for stuffed gefillte fish
2 Filling the carp skin with stuffing made of carp flesh

1

2
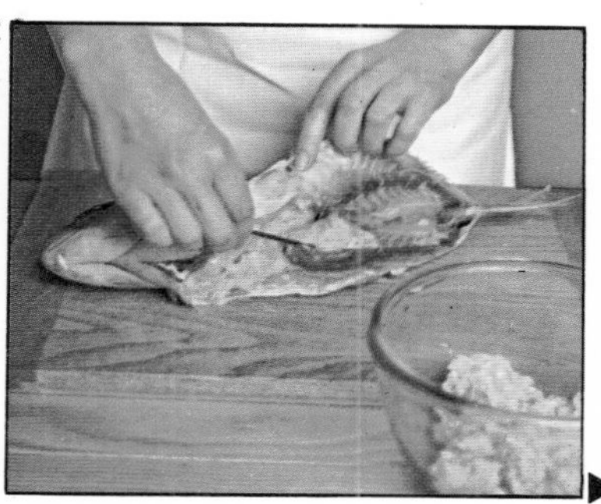

Gefillte fish continued

and poach for $1\frac{1}{2}$ hours.

Serve the stuffed fish cold, garnished with chopped aspic and bouquets of watercress and accompanied by chrane (see recipe on page 145).

A carefully skinned carp, stuffed and arranged with aspic and cress, is a traditional Passover meal

Fried gefillte fish

basic gefillte fish mixture
flour
oil (for frying)

To garnish
tomato slices
watercress

Method

Form the basic mixture into flat cakes $\frac{3}{4}$ inch thick and 2 inches in diameter. Roll in flour and fry the cakes in shallow hot oil until they are a deep golden-brown on both sides. Drain them well on absorbent paper. Serve cold, garnished with tomato and watercress.

Cheesecake

6 oz quantity of shortcrust pastry, or 4–6 oz biscuit crumbs mixed with 1–2 oz melted butter
3 eggs
8 oz caster sugar
$1\frac{1}{2}$ lb curd cheese
2 oz plain flour
$\frac{1}{4}$ pint double cream
pinch of salt
grated rind and juice of 1 lemon

7–8 inch loose bottom, or spring form, cake tin

Method

Line a greased baking tin with the shortcrust pastry or prepared crumbs. Set the oven at 350°F or Mark 4.

Place the eggs and sugar in a bowl and beat until light and creamy. In another bowl, thoroughly beat the cheese and flour; add cream, salt, lemon juice and rind. Combine the mixtures and again beat well.

Pour the mixture into lined tin and bake in the pre-set oven for $1\frac{1}{4}$ hours. Then turn off the oven and open the door slightly.

Take the cake out after 20 minutes. This keeps the cake, which rises in baking, from relaxing too quickly and thus becoming stodgy. This cake is best left overnight before cutting.

Coconut pyramids

8 oz desiccated coconut
4 oz caster sugar
2 eggs (beaten)

Method

Set the oven at 375°F or Mark 5 and grease a baking sheet. Combine all ingredients, then dampen your hands and form the mixture into pyramids, or flat cakes 2 inches in diameter and $\frac{3}{4}$ inch thick. Place these on the prepared baking sheet and bake in the middle to top of the pre-set oven for 20 minutes. Allow to cool, then store in airtight tins and use as required.

Sand cake

3 eggs (separated)
6 oz caster sugar
6 oz butter
4 oz potato flour
2 oz fine matzo meal
grated rind of 1 lemon

8-inch diameter cake tin

Method

Grease and line the cake tin. Set the oven at 350–375°F or Mark 4–5.

Beat the egg yolks and sugar together until light and frothy. Melt the butter, cool it slightly and add it to the egg mixture. Mix in the potato flour, matzo meal and lemon rind. Whisk egg whites until stiff and gently fold in. Pour into the prepared tin and bake in the centre of the pre-set oven for 1 hour. To test if done, push a fine skewer into the centre of the cake; it should come out clean.

Appendix

Notes and basic recipes

Almonds
Buy them with their skins on. This way they retain their oil better. Blanching to remove the skins gives extra juiciness.

To blanch almonds: pour boiling water over the shelled nuts, cover the pan and leave until cool. Then the skins can be easily removed (test one with finger and thumb). Drain, rinse in cold water; press skins off with fingers. Rinse, dry thoroughly.

To brown almonds: blanch, and bake.

To chop almonds: first blanch, skin, chop and then brown them in the oven, if desired.

To shred almonds: first blanch, skin, split in two and cut each half lengthways in fine pieces. These can then be used as they are or browned quickly in the oven, with or without a sprinkling of caster sugar.

To flake almonds: first blanch and skin, then cut horizontally into flakes with a small sharp knife.

To grind almonds: first blanch, then skin, chop and pound into a paste (use a pestle and mortar, or a grinder, or the butt end of a rolling pin). Home-prepared ground almonds taste much better than the ready-ground variety.

Apricot glaze
For use with all yellow fruit. Make a pound or so at a time as it keeps well. Store in a covered jar.

Turn the apricot jam into a saucepan, add the juice of $\frac{1}{2}$ lemon and 4 tablespoons water per lb. Bring slowly to the boil and simmer for 5 minutes. Strain and return to the pan. Boil for a further 5 minutes and turn into a jam jar for keeping. If for immediate use, continue boiling until thick, then brush amply over the fruit.

Breadcrumbs
To make crumbs: take a large loaf (the best type to use is a sandwich loaf) at least two days old. Cut off the crust and keep to one side. Break up bread into crumbs either by rubbing through a wire sieve or a Mouli sieve, or by working in an electric blender.

Spread crumbs on to a sheet of paper laid on a baking tin and cover with another sheet of paper to keep off any dust. Leave to dry in a warm temperature – the plate rack, or warming drawer, or the top of the oven, or even the airing cupboard, is ideal. The crumbs may take a day or two to dry thoroughly, and they must be crisp before storing in a jar. To make them uniformly fine, sift them through a wire bowl strainer.

To make browned crumbs: bake the crusts in a slow oven until golden-brown, then crush or grind through a mincer. Sift and store as for white crumbs. These browned ones are known as raspings and are used for any dish that is coated with a sauce and browned in the oven.

Chantilly cream
Whip a $\frac{1}{4}$-pint carton of double cream until just thickening; then add 1 teaspoon caster sugar and 2-3 drops of vanilla essence. Then continue beating until the cream holds its shape. (In warm weather and in a warm kitchen, if the sugar and essence are added before first whisking, it prevents cream getting thick.)

Chocolate caraque
Grate 3 oz plain chocolate or chocolate couverture (cooking chocolate). Melt on a plate over hot water and work with a palette knife until smooth. Spread this thinly on a marble slab or laminated surface and leave until nearly set. Then,

using a long sharp knife, shave it off the slab, slantwise, using a slight sawing movement and holding the knife almost upright. The chocolate will form long scrolls or flakes. These will keep in an airtight tin but look better when they are freshly made.

French dressing

Mix 1 tablespoon wine, or tarragon, vinegar with ½ teaspoon each of salt and freshly ground black pepper. Add 3 tablespoons of salad oil.

When dressing thickens, taste for correct seasoning; if it is sharp yet oily, add more salt. Quantities should be in the ratio of 1 part vinegar to 3 parts oil.

For **vinaigrette dressing** add freshly chopped herbs of choice.

Gelatine

As gelatine setting strength varies according to brand, it is essential to follow instructions given on the pack. For instance, Davis gelatine recommend 1 oz to set 2 pints.

Mayonnaise

2 egg yolks
salt and pepper
dry mustard
¾ cup of salad oil
2 tablespoons wine vinegar

This recipe will make ½ pint.

Method

Work egg yolks and seasonings with a small whisk or wooden spoon in a bowl until thick; then start adding the oil drop by drop. When 2 tablespoons of oil have been added this mixture will be very thick. Now carefully stir in 1 teaspoon of the vinegar.

The remaining oil can then be added a little more quickly, either 1 tablespoon at a time and beaten thoroughly between each addition until it is absorbed, or in a thin steady stream if you are using an electric beater.

When all the oil has been absorbed, add remaining vinegar to taste, and extra salt and pepper as necessary.

To thin and lighten mayonnaise add a little hot water. For a coating consistency, thin with a little cream or milk.

Eggs should not come straight from the refrigerator. If oil is cloudy or chilled, it can be slightly warmed which will lessen the chances of eggs curdling. Put oil bottle in a pan of hot water for a short time.

Watchpoint Great care must be taken to prevent mayonnaise curdling. Add oil drop by drop at first, and then continue very slowly.

If mayonnaise curdles, start with a fresh yolk in another bowl and work well with seasoning, then add the curdled mixture to it very slowly and carefully. When curdled mixture is completely incorporated, more oil can be added if the mixture is too thin.

Mussels

Mussels must be tightly closed before cooking. Examine carefully during the first thorough rinsing in cold water, and sharply tap any that are not tightly closed with the handle of a knife. If they do not respond by closing, discard them.

Scrub the mussels well with a small stiff brush and pull or scrape away any small pieces of weed from the sides. Rinse under a running tap, then soak them in a bowl of fresh water; do not tip this water off the mussels as this might leave sand still in them, but lift them into another bowl or colander and wash again. When thoroughly clean, lift them out and put into a large pan for cooking.

If mussels have to be kept overnight, store in a bowl without water in a cool place and cover them with a heavy damp cloth.

If storing mussels for a day or two, cover them with cold sea-water (if available) after washing and add a good tablespoon of oatmeal. This will feed them and keep them plump.

Pastry

French flan pastry

French flan pastry is made with plain flour, butter, caster sugar and egg yolks, and no liquid of any kind. The method of making is completely different from English shortcrust pastry and the dough should be firm and completely non-elastic. This means that the pastry keeps its shape during baking and when cooked is slightly short and melt-in-the-mouth. It should be made 1-2 hours before use, then chilled. Take it out of refrigerator 15-20 minutes before you use it and keep it at room temperature.

Basic recipe

4 oz plain flour
pinch of salt
2 oz butter
2 oz caster sugar
2-3 drops of vanilla essence
2 egg yolks

This quantity is sufficient to line a 7-inch diameter flan ring or 9-12 individual tartlet tins.

Note: 2 oz vanilla sugar may be used instead of caster sugar and vanilla essence.

Method

Sieve the flour with a pinch of salt on to a marble slab or pastry board, make a well in the centre and in it place the butter, sugar, vanilla essence and egg yolks. Using the fingertips of one hand only, pinch and work these last three ingredients together until well blended. Then gradually draw in the flour; knead lightly until smooth.

When coöled, French flan pastry is a delicate biscuit-colour; if over-cooked, it becomes hard and tasteless.

Genoese pastry

Basic recipe

$4\frac{1}{4}$ oz plain flour
pinch of salt
2 oz butter
4 eggs
$4\frac{1}{4}$ oz caster sugar

Method

Set the oven at 350–375°F or Mark 4–5; grease mould, line bottom only with a disc of greaseproof paper to fit exactly, grease again, dust with caster sugar, then flour.

Sift the flour 2 or 3 times with the salt. Warm the butter gently until just soft and pourable, taking great care not to make it hot or oily. Have ready a large saucepan half full of boiling water over which the mixing bowl will rest comfortably without touching the water.

Break the eggs into the bowl and beat in the sugar gradually. Remove the saucepan from the heat, place the bowl on top and whisk the eggs and sugar until thick and mousse-like. This will take 7-8 minutes and the mixture will increase in volume and lighten in colour; when lifted on the whisk a little will fall back, forming a ribbon on the mixture in the bowl. Remove the bowl from the heat and continue whisking for 5 minutes until mixture is cold. Now using a metal spoon, very gently cut and fold in two-thirds of the flour, then the butter, quickly followed by the remaining flour.

Watchpoint If you have an electric mixer, there is no need to place the mixing bowl over hot water but do add the flour by hand, cutting and folding it in as described in the recipe.

Turn the mixture immediately into prepared mould; bake in a pre-set oven for 30–35 minutes.

Sauces

Béchamel sauce

½ pint milk
1 slice of onion
1 small bayleaf
6 peppercorns
1 blade of mace

For roux
¾ oz butter
1 rounded tablespoon plain flour
salt and pepper

Method

Pour milk into a saucepan, add the flavourings, cover pan and infuse on gentle heat for 5-7 minutes. Strain milk and set it aside. Rinse and wipe out the pan and melt the butter in it. To give a white roux remove from heat before stirring in the flour. The roux must be soft and semi-liquid.

Pour on half of milk through a strainer and blend until smooth using a wooden spoon, then add rest of milk. Season lightly, return to a slow to moderate heat and stir until boiling. Boil for no longer than 2 minutes.

Watchpoint If a flour sauce shows signs of lumps, these can be smoothed out by vigorous stirring or beating with a sauce whisk, provided sauce has not boiled; draw pan aside and stir vigorously. It can then be put back to boil gently for 1-2 minutes before using. If it has boiled and is still lumpy, the only remedy is to strain it.

Demi-glace sauce

3 tablespoons salad oil
1 small onion (finely diced)
1 small carrot (finely diced)
½ stick of celery (finely diced)
1 rounded tablespoon plain flour
1 teáspoon tomato purée
1 tablespoon mushroom peelings (chopped), or 1 mushroom
1 pint well-flavoured brown stock (see page 156)
bouquet garni
salt and pepper

Method

Heat a saucepan, put in the oil and then add diced vegetables (of which there should be no more than 3 tablespoons in all). Lower heat and cook gently until vegetables are on point of changing colour; an indication of this is when they shrink slightly.

Mix in the flour and brown it slowly, stirring occasionally with a metal spoon and scraping the flour well from the bottom of the pan. When it is a good colour draw pan aside, cool a little, add tomato purée and chopped peelings or mushroom, ¾ pint of cold stock, bouquet garni and seasonings.

Bring to the boil, partially cover pan and cook gently for about 35-40 minutes. Skim off any scum which rises to the surface during this time. Add half the reserved stock, bring again to boil and skim. Simmer for 5 minutes. Add rest of stock, bring to boil and skim again.

Watchpoint Addition of cold stock accelerates rising of scum and so helps to clear the sauce.

Cook for a further 5 minutes, then strain, pressing vegetables gently to extract the juice. Rinse out the pan and return sauce to it. Partially cover and continue to cook gently until syrupy in consistency.

Stocks

Brown bone stock

3 lb beef bones (or mixed beef/veal)
2 onions (quartered)
2 carrots (quartered)
1 stick of celery
large bouquet garni
6 peppercorns
3-4 quarts water
salt

6-quart capacity saucepan, or small fish kettle

Method

Wipe bones but do not wash unless unavoidable. Put into a very large pan. Set on gentle heat and leave bones to fry gently for 15-20 minutes. Enough fat will come out from the marrow so do not add any to pan unless bones are very dry.

After 10 minutes add the vegetables, having sliced the celery into 3-4 pieces.

When bones and vegetables are just coloured, add herbs, peppercorns and the water, which should come up two-thirds above level of ingredients. Bring slowly to the boil, skimming occasionally, then half cover pan to allow reduction to take place and simmer 4-5 hours, or until stock tastes strong and good.

Chicken stock

This should ideally be made from the giblets (neck, gizzard, heart and feet, if available), but never the liver which imparts a bitter flavour. This is better kept for making pâté, or sautéd and used as a savoury. Dry fry the giblets with an onion, washed but not peeled, and cut in half. To dry fry, use a thick pan with a lid, with barely enough fat to cover the bottom. Allow the pan to get very hot before putting in the giblets and onion, cook on full heat until lightly coloured. Remove pan from heat before covering with 2 pints of cold water. Add a large pinch of salt, a few peppercorns and a bouquet garni (bayleaf, thyme, parsley) and simmer gently for 1-2 hours. Alternatively, make the stock when you cook the chicken by putting the giblets in the roasting tin around the chicken with the onion and herbs, and use the measured quantity of water.

Victoria sponge mixture

about 6 oz butter
about 6 oz caster sugar
3 large eggs
about 6 oz self-raising flour
pinch of salt
1-2 tablespoons milk

Deep 8-inch diameter sandwich tin

To make a good Victoria sandwich, weigh eggs in their shells and use exact equivalent of butter, sugar and flour.

Method

Grease and line sandwich tin; set the oven at 350°F or Mark 4.

Using the creaming method, soften the butter in a bowl, add the sugar and cream them together until soft and light. Whisk the eggs, add a little at a time and then beat thoroughly. Sift the flour with the salt and fold into the mixture a third at a time, adding enough milk to make the mixture drop easily from the spoon. Spread the mixture in the prepared tin and bake in pre-set oven for about 40-45 minutes.

Glossary

Baking Blind Pre-cooking a pastry case before filling. Chill pastry case, line with crumpled greaseproof paper and three-parts fill with uncooked rice or beans. An 8-inch diameter flan ring holding a 6-8 oz quantity of pastry should cook for about 26 minutes in an oven at 400°F or Mark 6. Take out paper and beans for last 5 minutes baking.

Blanch To whiten meats and remove strong tastes from vegetables by bringing to boil from cold water and draining before further cooking. Green vegetables should be put into boiling water and cooked for up to 1 minute.

Bouquet garni Traditionally a bunch of parsley, thyme, bayleaf, for flavouring stews and sauces. Other herbs can be added. Remove before serving dish.

Butter, clarified Butter which is heated gently until foaming, skimmed well and the clear yellow liquid strained off, leaving the sediment (milk solids) behind.

Butter, kneaded Liaison of twice as much butter as flour worked together as paste, added in small pieces to thicken liquid (usually at end of cooking process).

Cocotte 'En cocotte' implies that the food is cooked and served in the same round or oval ovenproof dish.

Compote Fresh or dried fruit poached in a syrup, usually of sugar and water.

Croûte Small round of bread, lightly toasted or fried, spread or piled up with a savoury mixture, also used as a garnish. Not to be confused with pie or bread crust (also croûte).

Croûton Small square or dice of fried bread or potato to accompany purée or cream soups.

Dégorger To remove impurities and strong flavours before cooking. It is done by sprinkling the sliced vegetable with salt, covering with heavy plate, leaving up to 1 hour, and draining off excess liquid.

Forcemeat (or farce) Savoury ingredients, eg. minced veal/pork, mixed with breadcrumbs or rice, vegetables, chestnuts, spices, and often bound together with eggs, milk or sauce. Used to flavour meat/poultry/fish; stuffed into cavities or between portions, or can be baked/fried separately and served with main dish.

Glaze 1 To make shiny with egg, water and sugar, or milk. **2** Jam or fruit glaze for coating sweets and cakes.

Julienne 1 A clear vegetable soup to which a mixture of finely shredded vegetables has been added.
2 The cut size and shape of vegetables and garnishes for certain dishes. A julienne strip is usually about $\frac{1}{8}$ inch by $1\frac{1}{2}$-2 inches long.

Marinate To soak raw meat/game/fish in cooked or raw spiced liquid (marinade) of wine, oil, herbs, and vegetables for hours/days before cooking.

Marmelade Fruit stewed and reduced until a thick, almost solid purée. Used as flan filling. Not to be confused with marmalade.

Poach To cook gently in trembling (not boiling) liquid – see **Simmer.**

Prove To leave shaped dough for a short period of rising before baking. This is carried out in a slightly warmer place than for general rising; for example over the stove or in a warming drawer, at about 80-85°F. Dough should be left for 10-15 minutes until it begins to swell.

Sauté To brown food in butter, or oil and butter. Sometimes cooking is completed in a 'small' sauce – ie. one made on the food in the sauté pan.

Salpicon mixture of diced/minced vegetables etc. used as a garnish on meat/fish dishes.

Scald 1 To plunge into boiling water for easy peeling.
2 To heat a liquid, eg. milk, to just under boiling point.

Shortening Fat which when worked into flour gives a 'short', crisp quality to pastry/cakes. Fats with least liquid, eg. lard, vegetable fat, contain most shortening power.

Simmer To cook in liquid at 195°F (91°C) or just below boiling point so that bubbles occasionally break surface.

Slake To mix arrowroot/cornflour with a little cold water before adding to a liquid for thickening.

Sweat To draw out flavour by cooking diced or sliced vegetables gently in a little melted butter in covered pan until softened (5-10 minutes).

Index